王正廷回顧録

Looking Back and Looking Forward
by
Chengting Thomas Wang

服部龍二 編

中央大学出版部

装幀　道吉　剛

編者はしがき

　中国の著名な外交官の一人に王正廷がいる。王正廷は，1920年代から1930年代初頭にかけて外交総長や外交部長を歴任し，日中戦争の初期には駐米大使を務めた。その王正廷の個人文書が，イェール大学の図書館に所蔵されている（Chengting Thomas Wang Papers, Manuscripts and Archives, Yale University Library）。王正廷の名前は，英語ではChengting Thomas Wangと表記される。イェール大学所蔵王正廷文書のなかで最も貴重なのが，Looking Back and Looking Forwardと題された王の回顧録にほかならない。

　王正廷の回顧録Looking Back and Looking Forwardは，英文の手書きで562頁となっている。この回顧録は，近代中国外交の重要文献として知られてきた。しかしながら，近年まで複写すら制限されていたこともあり，王の回顧録は広範に読まれてこなかったであろう。このため，顧維鈞のような中国人外交官と比べても，王の研究は知名度の割に遅れてきた感がある。本書は，王正廷回顧録Looking Back and Looking Forwardの全文を翻刻するものである。王正廷回顧録の目次は以下のとおりであり，その記述は外交関係に限らず出生から冷戦にまで及ぶ。

    PROLOGUE/　　Aim to Reach the Moon
     1/　　The Family Tree
     2/　　The Boyhood Days
     3/　　The Aspirations of a Youth
     4/　　Glimpses of American Life
     5/　　Chinese Students' Activities
     6/　　The 1911 Revolution
     7/　　The Evolution of the Revolution

8/ Comical Tragedy

9/ Interregnum

10/ The Paris Peace Conference

11/ Social Services

12/ The Good Roads Movement

13/ The Shantung Question

14/ In Troubled Waters

15/ The Northern Expedition

16/ Recovery of our Sovereignty Rights

17/ Dreams of an Industrialized China

18/ Continuous Growth of China

19/ Characteristics of the Chinese People

20/ A Woman's Place in China

21/ Chinese Conception of Religion

22/ Strong Love for Freedom

23/ Spreading of Christianity in China

24/ Freedom versus Communism

25/ Peering into the Future

それでは王正廷回顧録 Looking Back and Looking Forward には，いかなる内容が記されているのであろうか。回顧録の内容をふまえながら，王の足どりをたどってみたい。1882年に浙江省の奉化で生まれた王は，寧波の小学校で学んだ後に，西洋式の教育を受けさせたいという父親の意向で上海に渡り中英学校（Anglo-Chinese School）で英語を習った。次いで王は，天津の北洋大学に入学して法律を勉強したものの，義和団事件によって一時的に勉学を中断させられ上海に戻った。いったんは海関で働いた王だが，再度，天津の北洋大学を訪れてケント（Percy H. Kent）教授らのもとで法律を学んだ。天津に中英書院（Anglo-Chinese College）が設立されると，王はハート（S. Lavington Hart）に誘われて英文科の主任となっている。さらに王は，明徳学

堂という湖南省長沙の高等学堂で英文科主任としての職を得た。

　クリスチャンの家庭に生まれた王は，中国YMCAの活動にも関心を示した。王は中国YMCAの支部を東京に開設することに携わり，孫文とも東京で出会い中国同盟会に加わっている。他方でアメリカ留学を切望していた王は，1907年に渡米してミシガン大学で1年を過ごし，さらにイェール大学に進んだ。イェールでは，成績優秀を意味するファイベータカッパ（Phi Beta Kappa）を獲得した。

　1911年の辛亥革命後に王正廷は，南方派として南北和議にかかわり，暫定政府の組織を支えた。1912年に王は，唐紹儀国務総理のもとで工商部次長に任命され，1913年には参議院副議長となった。外交関係としては，1918年に広州政府からワシントンに派遣されている。1919年のパリ講和会議では，中国の全権を務めた。ワシントン会議後の1922年には，北京で山東条約の細目を日本と交渉した。1922年11月から翌年1月，1924年10月から11月，1925年12月から翌年3月には3回ほど北京政府の外交総長を務めたものの，外交総長の在任期間は最長でも3か月に満たなかった。

　この間の1922年12月から翌年1月に，王正廷は国務総理代理を兼任した。関東大震災時の中国人誤殺事件に際して，王は1923年12月に訪日しており，帰国後にはソ連との国交樹立交渉に従事した。1924年10月から11月には，財政総長を兼任してもいる。王は1928年6月から1931年10月，南京国民政府の外交部長を務めた。その在任期間は3年以上に及んだが，満州事変後に外交部長を辞した。

　1936年8月に王正廷は駐米大使に任命され，1938年9月までその座にあった。日中戦争初期のころである。そこへ胡適が新駐米大使としてワシントンに派遣されると，王は戦時下中国の首都となった重慶に帰国した。王は太平洋戦争の終結まで重慶にとどまっている。重慶で王は，中国紅十字会会長，交通銀行理事，フィリピン交通銀行理事，太平洋保健公司理事長などを務めた。終戦後には国共内戦のため1949年に香港へ渡り，そこで1961年に他界した。享年79であった。

　このように王正廷の活動は多岐にわたるのだが，なかでも最も注目に値す

iii

るのは外交関係であろう。1919年のパリ講和会議に中国全権として出席した王は、山東権益の対日譲渡を不服として、ドイツとの講和条約に調印しないことを主導した。他方で王は、ワシントン会議後の1922年に山東問題をめぐる日中交渉の中国側委員長に就任し、この問題に終止符を打ってもいる。ロシア通としても知られる王は、1920年代前半にソ連との国交樹立に努めた。すなわち王は、ソ連のカラハン（Lev M. Karakhan）らと交渉を進めたのだが、1924年5月に北京で中ソ国交樹立協定を締結したのは外交総長の顧維鈞であった。やがて1920年代後半に北伐が進展すると、北京政府に代わって南京の国民政府が中国の正統政府となった。

国民政府の外交部長に就任した王正廷は、アメリカ、イギリス、日本などの列国に対して国権回収を進め、中国の関税自主権を承認させるなどした。王は治外法権の撤廃をも強く求めており、その方策は「革命外交」ともいわれた。もっとも、「革命外交」を最初に唱道したのは王正廷ではなく陳友仁であり、陳友仁は広州国民政府の外交部長代理を経て武漢国民政府の外交部長となっていた。また、「革命外交」と称されていても、北京政府の「修約外交」を継承したところもあった。かつて北京政府も、列国との間で不平等条約の改廃を目標とする「修約外交」の機会をうかがっていたのである。他方で1929年に王は、張学良や蔣介石とともにソ連に対して東支鉄道の回収を試みて失敗した。この中ソ紛争は、奉ソ戦争とも呼ばれる。1937年から1938年にかけて王は、駐米大使として日中戦争初期にアメリカの世論に働きかけ、米中関係の強化に奔走した。

回顧録 Looking Back and Looking Forward で王正廷は、辛亥革命、パリ講和会議、山東問題、北伐、中国国権回収運動、日中戦争などを論じている。外交部長のころ、「アメリカ政府、とりわけアメリカの国民は、常に大いなる友情を中国に示していた」し、ランプソン（Miles W. Lampson）駐華イギリス公使は「知的かつ多才であり、完全なる対等を求める中国に同情的であった」と王は回想している。他方で王は、「対日政策には細心の注意を払った」という（本書131-132頁）。

そのような政治面だけでなく、天津や湖南における教育、さらにはアメリ

編者はしがき

カ留学を通じての文化交流などを知るうえでも，回顧録は有益となるだろう。アメリカ留学を切望していた王は，在米留学生の組織で会長となるなど学生活動に力を入れており，教育における体育の役割を強調したことも回顧録の特徴である。また王は，中国の科挙制度が廃止されて日露戦争に日本が勝利した1905年ごろを振り返っている。すなわち，中国の青年が日本に多く留学するようになった理由について，日本語と中国語には共通点が多く，訪日の費用も安いという2つを王は挙げた。

　加えて王正廷は，中国の宗教について少なからず記述を割いている。世界の5大宗教のうち，儒教と道教という2大宗教の起源が中国であることを王は誇りに思っていた。クリスチャンの家庭に生まれた王は，キリスト教を中国に広めることに熱心であった。訪日した王は早稲田大学の付近にYMCAの支部を開設しており，王が孫文と出会ったのも東京であった。中国の長い歴史や平和的な国民性についても王は自負しているものの，中国では識字率が低く，女性の地位も高くないことについては憂慮した。回顧録で王は中国悠久の歴史について語り，中国人の国民性は自由への強い愛着であると規定している。

　このように興味の尽きない王正廷の回顧録だが，事実関係では注意すべきところもある。例えば「田中上奏文（Tanaka Memorial）」について王は，「『田中上奏文』は日本による世界征服計画の青写真であった（Tanaka's secret memorial to his Emperor was the blueprint of Japan's plan for world domination）」と論じている（本書132頁）。しかしながら，「田中上奏文」の存在はきわめて疑わしく，王自身も「田中上奏文」が怪文書であることを知っていたはずである。「この本で前述したように」（本書25頁）というような表現が出てくることからしても，王は回顧録の公刊を意識していたと思われる。ただし，原稿の段階で絶筆となったためか，プロローグを含めて，文章や用語が十分に練られていない感もある。また，晩年の冷戦下で回顧録が記されたこともあり，王は中国内戦を「自由対共産主義（freedom versus communism）」とみなして台湾寄りの姿勢を示した（本書24章）。とはいえ，王が中国の将来的な発展に期待したことはいうまでもない。留意すべきところがあるにせよ，

v

中国の著名な外交官による歴史的証言として，王正廷の回顧録はやはり貴重なものであろう。

　王の遺族は1981年4月3日，英文で562頁に及ぶ回顧録などの王正廷文書をイェール大学に寄贈した。Looking Back and Looking Forward という回顧録の表題には，もともと A Plea for Freedom という副題が付けられていた。だがその副題は消されており，おそらく王自身によって削除されたのであろう。

　王正廷は回顧録を英文で手書きしているが，まれに中国語で補足してもいる。回顧録には誤字脱字のほか，下線が引かれたまま空欄で残されたところや，文法的に正しくないところもある。そのほか王正廷文書のなかには，手書きの回顧録をタイプ打ちしたものもあるが，タイプ打ちの文書にも誤記や脱字が多い。このため本書では，手書きの回顧録から原文の英語どおりに翻刻したうえで，さらにタイプ打ち原稿とも対照させ，必要に応じてルビを付けた。慎重を期したつもりではあるが，思わぬ誤りがありはしないかと懸念している。読者からの叱正を乞う次第である。

　末筆ながらイェール大学図書館は，複写ですら厳しく制限されていた王正廷文書の翻刻を認めて下さった。また本書は，2008年度の中央大学学術図書出版助成を得て刊行される。出版助成の審査に当たられた諸先生方や出版部，学事課などの関係各位に深謝申し上げたい。本書の刊行によって，王正廷や外交史の研究にわずかでも資するところがあるなら，望外の幸いとなるであろう。

　　2008年7月

　　　　　　　　　　　　　　　　　　　　　　　服　部　龍　二

Looking Back and Looking Forward by Chengting Thomas Wang

Index

編者はしがき

PROLOGUE/	Aim to Reach the Moon	1
1/	The Family Tree	7
2/	The Boyhood Days	11
3/	The Aspirations of a Youth	20
4/	Glimpses of American Life	37
5/	Chinese Students' Activities	47
6/	The 1911 Revolution	53
7/	The Evolution of the Revolution	62
8/	Comical Tragedy	68
9/	Interregnum	77
10/	The Paris Peace Conference	83
11/	Social Services	90
12/	The Good Roads Movement	97
13/	The Shantung Question	102
14/	In Troubled Waters	109
15/	The Northern Expedition	120
16/	Recovery of our Sovereignty Rights	128
17/	Dreams of an Industrialized China	137
18/	Continuous Growth of China	143
19/	Characteristics of the Chinese People	147
20/	A Woman's Place in China	152
21/	Chinese Conception of Religion	156
22/	Strong Love for Freedom	166
23/	Spreading of Christianity in China	173
24/	Freedom versus Communism	179
25/	Peering into the Future	185

王正廷回顧錄
Looking Back and Looking Forward

PROLOGUE

Aim to Reach the Moon

Many people have high aims in lift but are not willing to put in hard work in order to reach their goals. They have been dubbed as day dreamers. Yet the world's most famous explorers, inventors, discovers and founders of great institutions have come from the day dreamers. The fundamental difference between them is that the day dreamers continue to make dreams while the others convert dreams into realities.

Our own organization was brought into being by a coterie of such day dreamers fifty years ago. We are now celebrating its fiftieth anniversary. It would be well for us to give a short account of its origin and the aim of its organizers. To begin with they aimed at a brotherhood to cultivate that warm relationship and friendship that naturally exist between brothers of the same blood and to render help to each other, giving encouragement when and where it is needed.

At the Hartford (Conn.) Conference of the Chinese Student's Alliance in the fall of 1908 over a hundred students attended. They had come from universities and colleges located between Chicago and New York, but most of them were concentrated in educational institutions along the eastern border of the United States of America, such as Columbia, Yale, Harvard, Pennsylvania, and Princeton, just to mention a few, where the Chinese students were pursuing their studies abroad.

It was during this Conference when seven of us who had known one another before going to America, felt the need of banding together for a common objective in life. We had several informal talks when the Conference was not in session. Two of these brothers had since passed away. They were brother David Yui who was studying then at Harvard and brother S. C. Chu at Yale. An organization was the result and we called ourselves D & J, the David and Jonathon brotherhood, recalling the warm relationship and friendship between David, the lad, who was able to slay the giant Goliath, and Jonathon, the young son of King Saul. We began then to select and enroll in our brotherhood other young men of the right calibre, first among the Chinese students studying in the United States and later after returning to China we sought out the rising leaders of the country. Our brotherhood grew quite vigorously. Although separated from one another in our different walks of life we were able to keep in close contact with one another. Our annual Conventions afforded occasions to meet together, to compare notes and to give encouragement in our work.

In 1917 when I had an occasion to revisit American on a special mission for our government, I was given opportunities to meet in person the younger brothers who had joined us in the States. I came into contact with another organization in the States among our ever growing student population which had a similar objective as ours. After several meetings with their leaders we felt that our two organizations should merge into one. Such a merger was successfully effected with the approval of both organizations in their separate annual conventions that summer. From thence the name of the joint organization has been known as C. C. H., the full name being Ch'en Chih Hsüeh Hui (成志學會). As the name indicates, it is an association banded together to accomplish the purposes in life of its members, not only for each personal life but overall for our corporate life as a nation. Among the objects of our brotherhood is one "For the Uplift of China."

This objective is so high sounding and all inclusive that it has been even doubted by some of our own brothers whether we could ever achieve it. Some have gone so far as to call it a shot at the moon. Is it? Even as late as a decade ago the moon was considered too remote to be shot at. Now science has, however, made tremendous advances as to make it possible for us to take a trip to her. Some of us may even live long enough to take such a trip. Hence my entitling this short article as an "Aim to reach the Moon."

The aim to work for the uplift of our country is certainly a tremendous task. With one-sixth of the human population of the world and with a territory as large as, if not larger than, the whole of Europe, but with such a large percentage of our people being illiterate and with our standard of living as low as it is today, what a tremendous task we have to undertake to lift her up! We can take consolation in the thought that Rome — meaning of course the great Roman Empire — was not built in a day. Time is on our side. Besides, we have an enormous heritage, having existed as one nation for nearly fifty centuries in so far as our written history has recorded.

Now let us face this tremendous task. What are the essential objects of this task? First of all, we want to bring modern education to our people. I emphasize on the word modern. We have inherited a very high system of learning but it has been laying emphasis largely on literature and philosophy with a tincture of legal knowledge. The scholars, usually known as the literati, have always been treasured by the people, placed on the top of the social classes followed by the farmers, the artisans and the merchants. The literati, as a rule, have very little world possessions. Only the elite of them, who successfully passed the municipal, provincial and imperial examinations were awarded official positions which enabled them to enjoy lucrative incomes. Even at that they usually had very little wealth as compared with the merchants but socially they were at the top — the ruling class of the people. But what a small percentage they constituted among the population, less that 1%! The effect was a predominantly large number of the people being illiterate. They would tend to their farms or work with their hands. Only the merchants would seek sufficient learning to enable them to keep records of their business and carry on business correspondence.

With the introduction of modern education the situation is entirely changed. Besides literature, philosophy and law, knowledge in sciences is required for the engineers, doctors and other professions, while administrative and technical skills have to be acquired.

The first question I will ask of our brotherhood is how much have we done or are we doing in promoting modern education. This is a very wide and broad field. We do not have to be specialists to do it. Let us throw in our support to those who are doing actual educational work in any locality we happened to be placed.

The base of modern education is the necessity of giving elementary education to the masses of our people, particularly the farmers and the artisans who constitute over 80% of our population, the aim being to enable them to read and write. In other words a foundation is to be laid for them so that opportunities are given to them, either to pursue higher courses of study or at least afford them sufficient knowledge to read newspapers, pamphlets and other printed matters which tend to improve the work they are engaged in. In urging this program, I am not unaware of the overwhelming difficulties our country has to face in finding the resources to undertake it. From personal experience as well as by observing the work of others in promoting education for the masses, I am convinced that we have ample resources in our country for us to tap for this work. The vast amounts of money our people have the habit of spending for wedding and funeral occasions should and could be diverted into the channel for education. Moreover, municipal and provincial governments should be urged to set aside a fair percentage of the taxes for elementary and secondary education with substantial subsidies from the national government for this purpose.

What is most needed is a band of people determined to bring education to the whole nation. In this our brotherhood can make its contribution to propagate its work. Moreover, we have actually among us many distinguished educators. We are in fact carrying out another object of our organization, namely, to be mutually helpful in each others' life work by promoting education. We have lost such an educator in Dr. Chang Po-ling, the founder President of Nankai University who had built up the institution from Nankai High School for almost four decades of his life. Let us, one and all, contribute our share by promoting actively modern education for our people.

Another important and urgent problem facing our people is the promotion of physical education. There is no question about the virility of our race, otherwise we could not have lived so long, being one of the oldest, if not the oldest, nations of the world! As to number we decidedly outrank any other nation, having a population constituting one-sixth of the human family. To have virility is certainly a great asset but how to maintain it is an urgent problem. In the good old days — by that I am referring to an era some two thousand and more years ago — archery was one of the six "musts" in our educational program for boys. That connotates (connotes) physical education for our youths.

However, as cultivation of the mind gained a precedence over that of the body, gradually our people had been led to believe that physical strength was a mere mark of vulgarity for a scholar. The system of examinations introduced by the Court almost put an end to physical education, so much so that it was considered "nice and decent" for a scholar to wear long gowns and to have delicate hands with pointed finger-nails. That was the actual situation when I was admitted to Peiyang University in 1895. I was a weak and effeminate boy myself but I was not the only one. Most of my fellow school-mates were in the same condition. But Dr. C. R. Tenney, who was the President of the University, had the foresight to put in physical education and military drill as part of our curriculum. No one could pass on to a higher class without passing physical tests as well as other subjects. In a short time we began to put off our long gowns and cut short our nails. Personally, my health began to improve. In two short years I gained over a foot in height and half of my weight. Of course I was just at the age of growth but I firmly believe that but for this timely introduction of physical education in my life I would not have lived today.

Ever since my school days, I have therefore made it a habit in my life to keep up physical exercises. Moreover I put in a good deal of my thought and energy to the promotion of physical education in our country. It is a source of great satisfaction to witness the steady growth of our youths. As a rule the children grow up taller and stronger than their parents. I will therefore also urge my brothers to promote physical education as part of our work for the uplift of our country.

Important as modern education and physical health are in the life of a nation we will all agree that the most important is to bring happiness to our people. There are two ways. One is negative and the other is positive. The former deals with relief work for illness, calamity or any adverse circumstances while the latter is to direct one's mind from a mundane life to a spiritual outlook.

The old adage of "Sweeping the snow in front of your own gate but refraining from meddling with frost on other peoples' roof" is a warning against interfering with other people' business. But it tends to make people indifferent to the welfare of others. Frost does not do much harm to a roof, so the adage advises us not to meddle with it, but there are matters which are bound to do great harm if they remain unchecked. One could never feel indifferent if a case of cholera breaks out in the home of your neighbour or his house has caught fire. In such circumstances we should see to it that the patient suffering from cholera be placed in an isolation hospital and receive proper medical care, or we should at once call up the fire brigade to put the fire out. Hence the necessity of promoting Social Welfare work.

In the present day life there is a tendency for people to live in congested areas, creating thereby conditions which have to be carefully watched against any possible disaster. Epidemic outbreak, fire, robbery and street accidents are matters of great concern to the welfare of such communities. Above all there is always a concentration of poor people in large cities. Due to illness or unemployment people have been thrown out of work. Whatever may be the cause, the conditions of such people should be looked after by the social welfare workers. Let us join such work ourselves or else give our constant support to it.

The positive way of bringing happiness to our people has more far reaching effects than the negative way, although we should never neglect the latter work. As human beings we are constantly exposed to illness of one kind or another and illness is the main cause of other calamities that make us sad in life. But sadness or happiness in life is primarily a matter of the spirit. If we put less emphasis on the mundane life but more on the spiritual life, we will feel so much happier in our life.

History is abound with people who were in circumstances which would make them sad if measured by our mundane life. Confucius lauded one of his disciples for being able to live a happy life in the pursuit of knowledge with only a bowl of rice and a jug of soup for his daily food, while Jesus Christ commended the poor widow who gave two mites for the welfare of others. A bright spiritual outlook in life brings the greatest happiness to man, whatever be his race, colour or religion, and this spiritual outlook will only come from his religious devotion. I do not specify any particular religion, be it Confucianism, Taoism, Buddhism, Mohammedanism, or Christianity but all religions guide men towards that Supreme Being, the Creator of the Universe, the Word, the Tao, the Heaven, the Allah or whatever name is used to represent Him. To be able to lead our lives as well as others towards Him is and should be our greatest happiness in life.

Chapter 1

The Family Tree

We Chinese take a great pride in the family in which we are born. I do not believe that there is any other country where a family could be traced back to over two thousand years with a family tree giving the names of each generation, marking out those who had accomplished distinction, particularly in the field of literature and political achievements. The family of the K'ungs for instance keep a complete record from the time of Confucius, who was born in 551 B.C. or 2507 years ago. Confucius is a literalized form of K'ung Fu-tsze [sic], which means K'ung the master.

Of the hundred and odd families in China at least a quarter of them keep such records, but some of these records have been broken, not because due care was not taken in keeping them but because once an able descendant of another family succeeded in the overthrow of the ruling family and mounted the throne to rule the country in their stead. In most cases the descendants of the previous ruling family were mercilessly hounded out and duly executed. Some of them were lucky enough to escape detection but inevitably took on a different family name. This is generally known as a change of dynasty in China.

Seventeen dynasties have so far ruled China not counting the interregnum ones between some of these dynasties when the power of the new dynasty was not yet fully established and the old one had been overthrown. The K'ung family, I believe, holds the longest family record in that none of his descendants ever attempted to mount the imperial throne. I doubt that there was no one in the K'ung family who did not cherish such a desire to establish a new dynasty as several of them had shown great potential political prowess. The fact that their great ancestor had laid such emphasis on loyalty among the virtues to be achieved by man and that their family had inevitably been highly honoured by the reigning dynasties, such desire, though entertained by some of them, was never transformed into action. It was most fortunate both for the K'ung family in particular and our country in general that no attempt was ever made to seize the realm.

I recall that at an informal meeting of the revolutionary leaders after the overthrow of the Manchu dynasty in 1911 there was quite a strong sentiment to establish a new dynasty with Dr. Sun Yat-sen at the head. He was in every way qualified to be the founder of a new dynasty. It was through his life-long efforts to effect the overthrow of the Manchus that brought about their downfall. But Dr. Sun was adamant against such a move. Then it was suggested that the Duke K'ung, the 77th lineal descendant of Confucius, be crowned as the Emperor of this new dynasty. Out of profound respect for Confucius and the long established tradition of keeping the family out of politics, that suggestion was also dropped. It was then unanimously agreed that China should have a democratic form of government modeled after the United States of America.

I come from a family that keeps a full record for sixty-three generations. I am of the fifty-eighth generation, so there are five generations after me. I will be pointed out to a little boy at our village in Fenghua, Ningpo, Chekiang, as the great-great-great-grand uncle! I am a grandfather by my own right. My eldest granddaughter is now over twenty years old but she will be called great-grand aunt by that same little boy.

The Wang's constitute a very large family in China. It is said that out of every ten Chinese one is a Wang, so we are 45,000,000 strong. The name is often spelled Wong (王), especially in South China, and is not to be mistaken for other Wong (黃), which means, in English, yellow. Ours means king. In North China the latter is pronounced Huang.

There are two grand branches of the Wang family, the Lang-yieh (琅琊) Wang's and the Taiyuan (太原) Wang's, or we might say the Shantung Wang's and the Shansi Wang's. Our original ancestor first settled in Shantung province, the same province in which Confucius was born. After several centuries one of the Wang's moved to Shansi of which Taiyuan is the capital. From him came the Taiyuan Wang's.

The Wang family has had many of their sons attaining high scholarship. Many had passed the imperial examinations and were given important appointments in the government offices, several had

Chapter 1 The Family Tree

reached the highest position what is generally known in the West as premiership. Towards the end of the Sung dynasty, the Mongolian normads [nomads] were raiding the northern provinces of China and the situation deteriorated so much so that the Sung Emperors had to flee to South China for security. Two of them were actually captured by the Mongols. My thirty-sixth generation ancestor, that is twenty-two generations from me, followed the Court southward. He passed away during the flight in Hupeh province and his son continued to press southward but also died on the way in Kiangsi province. This ancestor had two sons, one was eleven years old and the younger seven. While they were in Kiangsi province, just to the south of Nanchang, its capital, they met a Mongolian horse brigade which cut across the refugees fleeing southward. The two little boys were in charge of a faithful servant who had held the hand of the younger brother. After the brigade had passed on the older boy could not be found, either he was killed in the melee, as many were hacked to death by the ruthless Mongols, or he must have escaped and gone on with the large crowd of refugees towards Kwangtung province. This servant decided not to follow this crowd for fear of further attack by the Mongols and turned eastward towards Chekiang. Finally he reached Fenghua in the district of Ningpo. The little boy in his charge was our ancestor in Chekiang, so this branch of our family has been living in that village for over six hundred years.

Here is where the value of the family record comes in. This servant, either through his own foresight or instructed by his master, had sewed the bulky record to his underwear and successfully carried it to the new abode. Knowing the danger of carrying such a record, he wisely put it in a Chinese wine jar and buried it in the ground over which he built a small temple for the worship of the local deity known as Tu-di (土地). To build a temple for Tu-di is a common practice of our villagers. After the Mongolian dynasty came into full power, he never revealed to anyone where the record was, even to his young master, until he knew he was soon to die. One day he led the young man to the spot where the temple was and unbosommed [unbosomed] the important secret with an urgent warning to keep it to himself, otherwise he and his children would be put to death by the authority serving the Mongols.

For nearly a century this secret was kept and only revealed by father to son, until our people regained their freedom from the Mongolian yoke at the downfall of the Yuan dynasty. During this century our ancestors were mere peasants, tilling the land for their existence, not daring to take up studies and aspiring to pass the imperial examinations for official appointments.

I mentioned about the older of the two boys who got separated from the servant after the Mongolian brigade drove into the crowd of refugees in Kiangsi. The boy was given up as either killed or lost. One day, some forty years ago, I happened to be visiting Mr. Wang Hsun (王勳), one of my old teachers, at his home in Shanghai. In the course of our conversation we touched upon the original home of our two families. I recounted to him the whole story as to how my family happened to settle down in Fenghua, Ningpo. To my great surprise he told me a parallel story about his family, which was first settled in Tung Kuan (東莞), Kwangtung province. His forefather was fleeing from the north together with a young brother under the care of a servant. They got separated when a Mongolian horse brigade drove past and he went straight south with the crowd of refugees and settled down in that distant province. For twenty generations they have made their home there. Unfortunately they did not have a family record of their ancestors prior to their sojourn to Kwangtung. It happened that a copy of the record was with the servant who guided the younger brother to Chekiang. Hence our branch of the Wang family in Fenghua, Ningpo, is enabled to trace back for nearly two thousand years without a break.

I have remarked in a paragraph above that the Wang's have always shown great intelligence and many of them have attained high scholarship. Dr. Wang Chung-hui (王寵惠博士), our leading jurist in China today, is a younger brother of Mr. Wang Hsun. He and I were schoolmates at the Peiyang University over fifty years ago while Mr. Wang Hsun was one of our teachers. Dr. Wang has attained world fame in law and jurisprudence. When studying in London after his graduation from Yale University, he had the German Civil Code translated into English and his translation is still being used as a text book in England. He has held many important positions in our government and is today the head of our Judicial Yuan, the highest legal organ of our country. He also served as a judge of the World Court at the Hague for a full term.

Chapter 2

The Boyhood Days

I was born to a Christian family, my father was a pastor of an Anglican Church for over three decades, and both my grandmother and mother were very earnest Christians. So it was fortunate that I got into contact with western influence early in my life.

After the fall of the Yuan Dynasty our family began once more to have their sons educated and to participate in the imperial examinations. With a Chinese on the throne they felt it was safe for their sons to reveal themselves from what stock they came and what positions their forbears had held in the government prior to the Yuan dynasty.

A century of peasant life did not seem to affect their intellectual prowess. Several succeeded in passing the imperial examinations and were awarded the degree of Chin-shih (進士) or doctorate. They were received in audience by the Emperor and given appointments in the government service. One of the Ming Emperors, after examining the records of our family, decreed that goods passing through our village should pay a small tax as a reward to the loyalty of the Wang family to the Sung Emperors. From that time on our family prospered again.

Unfortunately, the family life, like an individual life, is subject to its vicissitude. With the fall of the Ming dynasty and the enthronement of an alien Emperor, the fortune of the Wang's suffered a similar fate. They reverted once more to the life of peasants, eking out their existence by tilling the land again.

It was my grandfather who first broke away from our village in Fenghua and brought his children to the city life in Ningpo, where they came into contact with the Christian mission from England. My father was placed in a school, known as the Trinity College, where he distinguished himself as a scholar and orator but my grandfather died soon thereafter, leaving the children in care of my grandmother. She proved to be a very capable woman, working hard to be able to bring up her two boys and a daughter. Both boys graduated from the Trinity College.

I spent a good deal of my boyhood days with my grandmother as my mother had too much housework on her hand. Being a pastor's wife she had to provide for and help entertaining guests, especially on Sundays, besides caring for her every growing family. I am the fifth of her eleven children, but when I was a boy I had two older brothers and two order sisters and one younger sister and one younger brother. The older ones could fairly well take care of themselves while the younger ones claimed mother's special care. I was just at an age when a boy was most mischievous. As I look back in my life I cannot but realize how fortunate I am in having such a wonderful grandma. She was gentle and kind but quite firm in her control of me. She passed away when she was 83 years old.

I could not recall very distinctly of the years before I entered school at seven. The day I first went to school stands out as one of the milestones in my life. It has been the custom in our country for the new student to bring gifts to the old ones, in the form of cakes and a huge pot of sweetened tea. My father took me to the school and presented me to the teacher who happened to be my eldest brother. We went through the ceremony of presentation, as if the teacher was an outsider of the family. I made three "Kowtows" to him and then turned round to make three bows to my schoolmates. I had my new suit of dress on with new socks and shoes all made by my mother. It was a very colorful dress, consisting of a long silk robe in red and a black silk jacket. My shoes were also made of silk with the head of a tiger embroidered over the front of each shoe, showing the brilliant colors of a tiger's head. Mother must have bent over those shoes many late hours. That was one of my proudest days when I was made to feel that I was now on my way to achieve great things for my people and my country.

I studied four years under my eldest brother. Then father thought that I should have a western education, so I was sent to Shanghai under the care of my second brother who had studied at St. John's College, later known as St. John's University, and then working at the Chinese Maritime Custom in Shanghai. After tutoring me for about a year to give me rudimental knowledge of the English language, I entered the Anglo-Chinese School under Mr. Walter Moule, one of

Chapter 2 The Boyhood Days

the sons of Bishop Moule of our Church.

I was with this school for a little over two years when another momentous turn in my life occurred. The Manchu Court was much influenced by the advice of our two leading statesmen, Tseng Kuo-fan (曾国藩) and Li Hung-chang (李鴻章). It was through Tseng Kuo-fan that three groups of young boys of about forty in each group were selected and sent to America for western education, in the early eighties of the last century, in charge of Yung Wing, one of the first few chinese boys who graduated from Yale in 1852 over a century ago. Though the mission was recalled in 1881 these boys had acquired quite a working knowledge of what is known in China as "Modern" education. The traditional system of education channeled the youth largely along literary attainments as evidenced by the imperial examinations. The educated youth first went for the local examinations held in all prefectural cities. The successful candidates would have the privilege of attending the provincial examinations. Finally an imperial examination would be held in the national capital for those who had passed the provincial tests. The first degree was known as Hsiu-tsai (秀才) corresponding to the western degree of Bachelor of Arts or its equivalent, the second as Chü-jen (舉人) or Master of Arts, and the last one as Chin-shih (進士) or doctorate. Finally the Emperor would personally supervise the selection from among the Chin-shih a number of the best in scholarship and penmanship and appointed them Han-lin (翰林) and admitted them to the College of Han-lin, the highest institution of learning in the country. The Han-lin's were the elite of the land honoured and reverenced throughout the country. Important government positions were conferred upon then and were always on the priority list.

This system of examinations had proved to be of an immense value to the country, in that the best brains were employed for the governing of the nation. The fact that for over thousand years it was maintained through the various dynasties, proved its efficiency and won the approval of the whole people. But it had three vital defects.

In the first place, the number of successful candidates for each of the three tests was limited as prescribed by the government, irrespective of the number of candidates who attended the examinations. It is self-evident that good scholarship could not flourish at an even rate at the various periods when examinations were held. So it happened

13

quite often that sometimes a large number of excellent scholars failed to be among the successful candidates because of the prescribed number, while at other times, many of the successful ones proved to be of inferior caliber.

Secondly, the tests were mainly on literary basis. Human intelligence is so diversified that the best brains do not show themselves in one line of knowledge. In our early history some of our ancestors had distinguished themselves in science, arts, medicine, engineering, mathematics and other forms of knowledge. They were in the days before this system of examinations was instituted. I firmly believe that the present lack of good scientists, artists, doctors, engineers, mathematicians, etc, is largely the resent of this system. That is why the country at the end of last century was so deficient in men capable to compete with the west along other lines than literary attainments, important as these are and ever will be.

Lastly, scholars do not always have executive ability. They may be excellent in the production of literature, compose beautiful poems, and write brilliant themes, but these do not necessarily qualify them to be appointed magistrates, governor, and state councilors. They often prove to be pedantic, dreamy and inefficient in the management of local, provincial and state affairs.

Towards the last three decades of the 19th century there was a strong growing sentiment that China must have "reforms." Tseng Kuo-fan, who had won great fame as the statesman who succeeded in coping with and defeating the Tai-ping rebellion in the middle of that century, was the first one to recognize the importance of knowing and understanding the Western nations. He believed that the best way was to select youths in the formative age between twelve and sixteen to be sent to America, England and other European countries. He succeeded in sending such youths to America. Financial stringency of the country then only enabled him to send three such groups of about forty in each group to America. His other plans had to be laid aside. Even these groups could only be maintained for about eight to ten years. After he stepped out of the government the Education Mission was recalled. Several of these boys were already in American universities while others had finished their high school courses. It was indeed most unfortunate that so few had been sent to America and they were not given an opportunity to complete their studies. Plans

Chapter 2 The Boyhood Days

for Education Missions to other countries had to be abandoned. What a world of difference would China have been, had Tseng Kuo-fan's plans been carried out in their entirety! Yet though few in number, these youths had played a great part in awakening our country to the importance of renovating our system of education.

So it came about that after our war with Japan in 1895, the government decided to introduce a new system of education by establishing universities with various branches of learning. The first university of this kind was founded in Tientsin, the chief trading port in North China. There were no students qualified to take up courses in the university proper and it was found necessary to have a preparatory school to start with. But there were still too few in North China who had sufficient knowledge to be so enrolled. Dr. Charles D. Tenney, an American missionary, was appointed, as the President of the new institution with Mr. Tsai Shao-ki, one of the 120 youths who were sent to America under the Education Mission, as the Director. They knew that our youths in South China were better qualified to take up courses which were taught in English. So they went south and held two examinations, one in Shanghai and the other in Hongkong. In order to encourage students to join this "modern" institution, it was wildly published that they would get free board and tuition together with free textbooks and stationeries, besides, each student would get a monthly allowance for expenses from one tael up to seven taels, one tael being worth at that time about eighty cents United States currency.

My father received a comparatively small salary as the pastor of a church, so could not afford to let me have a Western education abroad, but he entertained a deep belief that such education would be of tremendous value to our people and country. The prospect of getting it through this new university prompted him to urge me to try this examination to be held in Shanghai. I was fortunate in passing it with the second year grade of the preparatory school. Besides free board and tuition, I would also receive a monthly allowance of one tael and half. The first year grade students would get one tael. Those in the third and fourth year grades two taels and two taels and half respectively. Those who finally reached the university grade would be given from four to seven taels a month as they advanced in their studies. Father was overjoyed on my success, so was I. Nothing could kindle a greater fire in youth than the prospect of a new adventure. So was mother. She must have spent many late hours again to get ready my new wardrobe. Unexpectedly, strong opposition came from my grandmother and maternal grandmother, that is, my mother's mother. They both had a tender spot in their hearts for me, particularly my own grandmother. She had taken such good care of me when I was a small boy before I went to Shanghai to study and Shanghai is quite near to Ningpo. To them who knew practically nothing about China's geography, thought of Tientsin as a distant land. I was only fourteen years old then and had always been sickly from boyhood days. They upbraided my father for being so hard-hearted as to allow such a small boy to go so far away from home with not a single relative to look after me.

According to Chinese filial piety no son or daughter could or should argue or answer back when admonished by a parent, even when he or she had a family of their own. So father gave a diplomatic answer that he would send for me to return home from Shanghai to be personally questioned by them as to whether it was my own wish to proceed to Tientsin. The two ladies had thought that father was the culprit as if to banish me from kith and kin. After my return to Ningpo without saying a word to me as to what had happened between them, I was brought one day into their presence when my maternal grandmother came to our home for their questioning. Not realizing what the two grandmas had in mind, when they asked me as to whether it was my wish to go so far away as Tientsin in order to get an education, I was so enthusiastic over my prospect of having a new adventure that I just bubbled over it. Father was keeping a straight face without making any comment either in support of his own-views or theirs. I noticed the two ladies just exchanged glances at each other and them my own grandmother simply remarked that she would pray for me in her daily prayers and trusted that I would study diligently and be a good boy. This episode has left a deep mark in my mind. As I grow older I see more distinctly the beauty of Chinese family life.

Soon thereafter I embarked on my new adventure. Mr. Tsai Shao-ki, our Director, accompanied a batch of 27 students on board a Chinese steamer by the name of "Hsin-yu." Luck would have it that there was a storm in the open sea beyond the Yangtze River. Our little steamer of some 2,000 tons had to be anchored at its mouth. It rocked and rolled so much so that we were very seasick. I was among four boys in our cabin all of the age between fourteen and sixteen. We did cry like babies! After a few hours the Captain thought the storm had died down sufficiently for his ship to weigh anchor but the sea was still as rough as could be. We had no food for three days but moaning as if we were dying. None of us had ever traveled on the open seas before. The first port we touched on our way to Tientsin was Chefoo. The funny thing about seasickness is that soon after a ship enters a port all the sufferings are gone. Mr. Tsai had the paternal instinct to invite all his protégés to a tea party in the parlour of the ship. We were as happy and gay as ever.

We were the first batch of students to arrive at our new seat of education. To our surprise the servants outnumbered us but of course they were employed for the whole batch of students. None of our batch knew the northern dialect, so for the first few days we conversed with them more or less by sign language. Soon thereafter other batches joined us, some from local places and others from as far as Canton in the south. Towards the end of 1895, our regular class work began. The degree of advancement in the different sections of the country in Western education was very evident. The Cantonese, who had the earliest contact with the West were in the upper classes while those from mid-China and the northern provinces in the lower ones. During the first year all the students were only qualified to pursue courses in the Preparatory Department of the University. The school year did not begin in the fall and end in June as generally practised in Western countries. Ours began with the Chinese New Year, round about the first part of February according to the solar calendar, so at the end of each lunar year those students who succeeded in completing their courses were duly promoted to a higher class. University proper had its work started by the beginning of the next year with three faculties, arts, law and engineering. Most of the professors of the University were engaged from America and England.

For the four and half years nothing unusual had happened. Regular routine class work was being carried on without any interruption but a big storm had been gathering momentum, culminated in the early summer of 1900, which nearly killed this new institution. At least it caused a suspension of its work for nearly five years. More will be said in a later chapter about this political storm, generally known as the Boxer Outbreak.

There was, however, one outstanding feature in our modern education which must be pointed out here. Hitherto the object of education in China was to train a youth along the intellectual lines with a moral background. In other words, it aimed to bring out in him his intellectual powers with a view of using them for the good of his country and people. Very little attention was given to his physical development, although archery was one of the six requirements in a boy's education in the old days. By archery it was meant to develop the boy physically as well. However, this practice was gradually abandoned until a student would feel ashamed to be among those who have great physical strength. It came to be considered as "ungentlemanly" to have such strength.

Dr. Tenney had been in China long enough to understand why Chinese youths were averse to physical exercise. Besides introducing western games, such as football and basketball, he had instituted a number of athletic activities. To his dismay he only found a handful of his students to be interested in them. So he started something that was distinctly novel to the Chinese students at that period. It required much courage to undertake it. He introduced military drill as part of the curriculum. All the boys had to take weekly drills with an instructor from the American navy to teach them not only drill, but also the art of war. The latter proved to be the trump card. Although they hated to take on military drill as beneath their dignity but they did want to make China strong militarily. Hence their willingness to take up the drill. At first they were given dummy rifles, but as they progressed in the art of handling rifles and as they grew in age, they were given real ones. Later, they were even trusted with genuine shots for target practices.

This innovation of an age-long ideal of "a sound mind in a sound body" has brought about revolutionary changes in the life of our students. Those who have been benefited by open-air exercises found themselves in the best of health. I was one of these. Being sickly in my life up to the time I went to Tientsin, I was a frail boy, short in stature and poor in health. On my second visit home, that is, two years after I was in the "new" school, I grew so much and so strong as to astonish my mother, who had to make new clothes for me not only longer but broader. As I look back in my life I consider that to have good health is the greatest blessing of a mortal being. Because of this conviction I have thrown myself whole-heartedly to the promotion of athletics. I have been telling our youth that they should start early in making "deposits" in the "Bank of Health" in order to draw best "dividends" throughout their lives. The "deposits" are in the form of daily open-air exercises and the "dividends" in the form of robust health will automatically come to them.

My student life at the Peiyang University was abruptly brought to an end in the early summer of 1900 when the so-called Boxer Outbreak raised its ugly head. It also marks the turning point in the internal life of our country, the making of a Republic in place of an age-old Monarchy, as well as her relation with the other nations of the world with a policy of international cooperation in place of isolationism. These will be touched upon in later chapters. It also brought an end to my boyhood days.

Chapter 3

The Aspirations of a Youth

When my school life was abruptly cut short by the Boxer Outbreak in 1900, I was at a loss to know where to continue my studies. Our University had to suspend its work altogether. Allied military forces were being landed at Taku at the time when we were ordered by our school authorities to leave for our homes. The aim of the Boxer Movement was to drive all foreigners from China. Their slogan was to "Back up the Manchus and destroy the foreigners." It was a patriotic attempt to get rid of the threat of some of the western nations to enslave China. The country had already been allotted to be divided among the western Powers, marked out by what was known as the Spheres of Influence (勢力範圍), and "Partition of China" seemed to be inevitable. The motive of the movement was decidedly patriotic and would certainly receive the support of the Chinese people, had the right means been used to reach its objective. But the Manchu court was woefully lacking in statesmanship at that period. In fact after the abortive efforts of Emperor Kwang-hsü to bring about fundamental reforms for the country, he himself was being held a prisoner in the palace and men of ability in the government were relieved of their posts, while several actually lost their lives. The power of the government was vested in the vain Empress-Dowager surrounded by a number of hot-headed inexperienced young Manchu princes.

The Manchu dynasty was always looked upon as an alien rule by the Chinese people, but the first few Emperors were men of great wisdom who knew how to share the management of the government with the Chinese. Nominally the Manchu Emperor was on the throne but actually most of the important government offices were held by the Chinese. When the Boxer Movement was gaining momentum in north China, the Empress-Dowager thought that she could make use

Chapter 3   The Aspirations of a Youth

of it to further tighten her powers over the Emperor. The movement was led by some religious fanatics who believed that by means of incantation their men were impregnable to bullets and gun shots. Hence with fistic jiu-jitsu and swords they could overcome soldiers with rifles and guns.

In the early summer of 1900 the Court decided to launch the Boxer Outbreak in Peking by attacking the much hated Foreign Legations. The German Minister and a secretary of the Japanese Legation were the first victims of the attack. The guards of the various Legations were called upon to protect the Legation quarters when it was surrounded by the Boxer forces. An imperial edict was issued by the Court to all viceroys, governors and magistrates throughout the country to "put to death" all foreigners within their jurisdiction. Had the edict been despatched in its original form, what a carnage would have been the result! What the consequences would have been could only be left to imagination. But there were three men in the Foreign Office who knew what the consequences would be by issuing such a reckless edict. They were in charge of despatching it by telegraph, which being new and foreign, was assigned to the Foreign Office. They had the courage to change the words "put to death" into "protect." Of course this was later detected and the men paid their lives for this courageous act. The edict in its original form was again despatched but it had lost its spontaneity, besides most of the viceroys and governors knew what the consequences would have been, should they follow the later instructions. So nonchalantly they obeyed the first instructions and ordered that all foreigners be PROTECTED.

While the Legation quarters were being besieged, allied forces fought their way to Peking. The Boxers found themselves riddled by bullets and gun shots, and the whole movement collapsed like match boxes. The Court had to flee from Peking to Sian and sue for peace. The ensuing peace treaty was in most humiliating terms. Besides exacting a huge sum from the Chinese government, known as the Boxer Indemnity, other concessions were wrung from China, among them being that the area in which my University was situated was made into a German Concession and its property and equipment were taken over. It looked as though that the life of the University had ended.

It also looked as though my own school days were over. I had passed out of the teen-age and was a young man of excellent health with broad shoulders and deep chest, the results of my athletic activities at the University. Young men always have day dreams. I had mine. I knew that my father did not have the means to give me an education abroad, although he would have wished so much to see me get it. My dream was that I should save sufficient fund to defray my traveling expenses and at least sufficient for the first year. Then I would work through college as many American young men do under similar circumstances. The question was how to find a job that would give me a remuneration whereby I could have a balance large enough to permit me to accumulate this fund. It was a wild dream, as jobs of that kind were not easy to find. It is not easy to get nowadays either.

The first opportunity came in the spring of 1901 when the Chinese Maritime Customs called for clerks through competitive examinations. I applied for and passed them and was assigned to the Assorting Department of the service in the Shanghai office. The pay was twenty-five taels or roughly forty Mexican dollars. That was considered a very good job. I could have saved half of my pay but it would have taken ten years to enable me to have a sufficient fund to realize my dreams, besides the work in that department did not interest me. It was largely routine work with practically nothing to add to my knowledge. I had started my second year law at the University under Professors James and Kent, two brilliant British teachers. When the University suspended its work, Professor James had returned to England but Professor Kent remained in Tientsin and started practicing law. So I wrote to him whether there was an opening in his office to work as a clerk and at the same time to continue studying law under him. To my great delight he gave me an appointment in his office with a promise to give me legal instructions. Immediately thereafter I resigned from my customs post and went up to Tientsin to resume my studies. Mr. Kent gave me not only an office but living quarters free of charge. I was therefore enabled to continue on accumulating my savings for the realization of my dream.

I was with Mr. Kent for nearly two years, enjoying my work immensely which consisted mostly in translating Chinese documents into English and vice-versa, besides studying law courses under his instructions and tutorship. I would have stayed with him for some years until my savings should be sufficient to enable me to study

Chapter 3 The Aspirations of a Youth

abroad. I was fully conscious that it might have taken five or six years to do so.

However, an offer came from quite an unexpected quarter, with a salary almost five times of what I was getting. Eager as I was to shorten the time to embark on my study abroad, I was rather hesitant to leave Mr. Kent. He was such a good employer and teacher, so I boldly took him into my confidence. The offer came from Dr. S. Lavington Hart, a missionary of the London Mission, located in Tientsin. He was starting a new educational institution, to be known as Anglo-Chinese College, and was looking for suitable teachers. I did not realize then that it was Mr. Kent who recommended me to Dr. Hart. So in our interview Mr. Kent not only did not object to my leaving his office but actually strongly advised me to accept the offer together with his assurance that he would continue to supervise my law courses prescribed by him. I was really jubilant over this turn of affairs which raised my status to a teacher, a position always highly respected in China.

My father was getting on in years and rather poorly in health. Like all Chinese fathers he was anxious that I should get married. He had hinted that several times since I left Peiyang University. He knew I was deeply in love with a cousin of mine, Mary Sze. In fact being cousins we were thrown together since babyhood and our love was not only "love at first sight" but seemed to have been pre-ordained. As I was bent on getting a full education, I did not deem it wise to have a family on my hand, so I warded off father's suggestion by saying that a man should have a lifelong work first before he should get married. I was only a student while working in Mr. Kent's office.

My promotion into the class of a teacher gave father an opportunity to renew his suggestion. In fact it was couched in the form of a paternal order. "There are three forms of being unfilial, and the greatest of them is the one leaving no descendants to perpetuate the family," so he quoted from Chinese classics. To this I had nothing to say, so it was arranged to have my marriage solemnized during my summer vacation in 1902. After our marriage I confided to Mary of my great desire to get a full college education in America. She saw at once the importance of my plan, though it was still nothing but a dream. She pledged me her full support and would give it to help me to realize my objective. I will say without any quibble that happy is the man

23

whose life mate sees things eye-to-eye with him. She willingly agreed to stay with my parents while I returned to Tientsin to teach. This would lessen my expenses, so I was able to continue piling up my savings against Der Tag as the Germans would say. For five years Mary and I played the role of two famous Chinese mystical lovers, the Cow Boy and the Weaving Maid, who only meet once a year over the Milky Way (天河, 鵲橋) and that on the night of the 7th day of the 7th moon! Only we were able to spend more than a month together every summer, and sweet were our annual reunions! It is said that distance makes the hearts grow fonder, to which I fully subscribe. I will add that reunions after self-imposed separation render out hearts so much the fonder.

I spent two happy years at the Anglo-Chinese College. In Dr. Hart I found one of the best educated men I have ever met. He had three A's to his credit at Cambridge University in Science, Mathematics and Literature. In addition he was an excellent theologian, whose sermons I thoroughly enjoyed. He was also quite proficient at the piano. Indeed he was a man of great versatility. My own life has been much enriched because of my association with him. I would have stayed on indefinitely with him, were it not for my burning desire to get an education abroad. As opportunities came my way for the realization of that objective, I had to make two more changes and each change brought me nearer to my goal.

Besides Dr. Hart and myself (me) we had several others on our teaching staff. While teaching we absorbed a good deal of knowledge in the management of students and in keeping up abreast with the political developments of the country. Teaching in itself is really a most fascinating employment. The teacher has under him boys of an age whose future is in the making. Naturally their first object is to get knowledge, but how to guide them into the right path of living and how to promote their physical welfare are also parts of an all-round education. While a student myself at Peiyang, I was much impressed with the work of the Young Men's Christian Association. Its symbol of an inverted triangle and with Mind and Body forming the two arms of the triangle and with spirit at the base expresses most realistically its object. The Y. M. C. A. work was just being started in the cities of China, although in most of the Mission Schools there were already in existence organizations of this nature but rather loosely related with

Chapter 3   The Aspirations of a Youth

one another.

I was a charter member of the Tientsin Y. M. C. A. before the Boxer Outbreak and resumed my activities of the Association on my return to Tientsin. When I took up my teaching work at the Anglo-Chinese College I considered that my duties as a teacher should not be confined in the classrooms only. It was for me to throw my influence with the boys in the development of their character and their physical well-being. In these efforts I feel that I am well rewarded with the type of men in the various walks of life in China today who were once my pupils.

There was another angle of my life that first found an expression while teaching at the Anglo-Chinese College. It was a political one. My study of the American Revolution coupled with what I had learned from our family record, the inherent love for freedom was kindled within me. Twice in the history of China, we had two alien dynasties, Yuan and Ts'ing. What horrible sufferings my ancestors had received at the hand of the Mongols! When Taiyuan was taken by them, several thousands of the Wang's were massacred by them, including the aged, women, and children for we were staunch supporters of the Sung Emperors. A few managed to escape from their crutches and the grandfather of my ancestor who settled in Ningpo was among them, that little boy who got separated from his brother but saved and protected by the faithful servant of the family whose story I told in a former passage of this book. The Yuan dynasty lasted for about a century when they were driven out by loyal Chinese under the leadership of Chu Yuan-chuang who eventually founded the Ming dynasty. But by the middle of the 17th century there were constant incursions from the Manchus, culminated in the founding of the Ts'ing dynasty with Manchu Emperors on our imperial throne. Many attempts had been made to overthrow them, the last one before the successful revolution under Dr. Sun Yat-sen was the so-called Taiping rebellion which nearly upset it. Since the establishment of this dynasty all males of the Chinese people were forced to wear what was generally known as the queue but more popularly known as the "pigtail." It was a badge of servitude to adopt the Manchu style of hairdressing. At the capitulation of the Ming forces certain terms were agreed to by the leading General of the Ming army, Gen. Hung Ch'eng-ch'ou, one of them being that all adult Chinese males had to wear the queue, although boys could still use the Ming style of both dress and hair-dress and the grown-ups could revert to the Ming style after death. That is why all Chinese males during the Ts'ing dynasty were laid away in their coffins with full Ming dresses and headgears. Chinese females, however, were never subjected to this humiliation. Throughout the Ts'ing dynasty they dressed exactly as their female ancestors did before then.

One of my colleagues at the Anglo-Chinese College, Mr. S. F. Chien, and I were very intimate friends, in fact he was one of my schoolmates at Peiyang. The more we discussed the question of wearing the queue, the more indignant we became. Finally we made a pact to have this badge of servitude cut off and to resort to the western style of hairdressing together with the western dress. We were not fully aware that we were liable to have our heads cut off also! But like all young men we were impetuous. So one day we had our queues removed when our western dresses were ready and boldly appeared at the morning service of our College. Dr. Hart was conducting the service. I am sure he was aware of our new apparel but being a gentleman of a liberal mind he did not show any sign of approval or disapproval and the service was conducted in the usual manner. But we were quite conscious ourselves. As the teachers sat at the front row, we felt as if all the eyes of over one hundred boys were riveted on our heads.

In this connection I must relate the acute reaction to my aged father. On hearing what I did to my queue and knowing the danger I was exposed to, he wrote me such a long letter admonishing me of my wrongful action, and being quite a good Chinese scholar, he quoted classical parts to back up his statements, that I felt I had no leg to stand on. So I wrote him one of my shortest replies : "I am very sorry, father, for what I did, but it is already done." Both to ease his mind and a host of anxious friends and relatives, I had a false queue made and sew it on to my hat, so that on certain occasions I again dressed like all my compatriots including the "badge of servitude," but I had made up my mind never to rear a real queue.

Just as I was enjoying my work at the College, a new turn came to my life in a most unexpected way. China is really a huge country. Most of the twenty-four provinces composing it then is(are) larger than any country in Europe, excepting Russia, but our largest province,

Chapter 3 The Aspirations of a Youth

Szechuan, is larger than the European Russia. The inhabitants of these provinces differ very much from one another in their characteristics, just as the component parts of Europe have their different characteristics. Only in Europe they are known as different nations. In China it is one nation, with peculiar characteristics in each of the provinces.

Hunan is one of the twenty four provinces with a population of 28,443,279. The Hunanese are noted for their strong headedness. They have furnished some of the greatest statesmen, generals and administrators of the country. Our distinguished statesman, Tseng Kuo-fan, who saved the Manchu dynasty from the Taiping rebels and who sent the three groups of Chinese students to America was a Hunanese. Up to the time of the Boxer Outbreak, the Hunanese were the leading reactionaries against any foreign intercourse. They believed in isolationism. However, after the allied forces took over Peking and exacted those humiliating terms in the peace treaty, our Hunanese compatriots suddenly awakened to the danger of isolationism and decided to bring in modern education to their province. Like all strong-headed people they did not believe in half measures. All of a sudden they were in the foremost calling for reforms in all directions. The provincial government set aside large sums of money for the establishment of modern educational institutions throughout the province. A High School was planned in Changsha, its capital, with a view of developing it into a university in due course of time. So emissaries were dispatched to places like Tientsin where modern education of university standard was in full bloom. One of these emissaries called on me and asked me to take up work at the High School as the head of the English department. I was rather reluctant to leave the Anglo-Chinese College, besides Hunan is rather far from the coast of China. His insistence and the lure of adventure finally won over me. In the early spring of 1904 I left Tientsin for the second time on one of the Kailan Mining Company's boats, sailing for Shanghai. The boat touched at Port Arthur on her way south. She was actually anchoring in the port when a Japanese attack came. The Russians, who had control of the port, having wrested it from China, were caught unaware on the night of February 4th. Several of her warships were damaged and disabled by the silent torpedoes fired at them just outside the port when the forts opened fire in great vehemence but I

27

am sure without hitting any of the Japanese ships. Next day the Japanese came to attack again in full naval force and exchange of gun fire lasted for over an hour. This was my first experience in having shots fired over our heads and dropping in the water with great splashes. Fortunately none of the shots hit our boat. Two days later we were allowed to sail out of the port but a deplorable incident happened while passing through the narrow neck at the entrance of the port. Through some misunderstanding between the port authorities and the fort commander, three shots were fired at us just above the water line. One of these shots hit a boy in the cabin next to mine and tore off one of his legs. The ship had to detour her course so as to enable her to land the poor suffering boy at Weihaiwei for medical treatment. Weihaiwei was then in British control, having leased it from China. The two ports are opposite each other with the body of water known as the Gulf of Pechili between them. I have never been able to find out whether the lad had survived his operation.

Before I took up my new post in Changsha, I spent a short holiday with my parents and my "Weaving Maid" who was expecting her first baby. I then sailed up the Yangtze $\overset{R.}{\text{river}}$ on a small river boat and boarded a still smaller one at Hankow for my new destination. I did not know what was in store for me, only I felt that God was guiding me towards my goal for a full college education.

Changsha is a typical provincial capital and is the seat of the governor. There is a big lake between the two provinces, Hupeh and Hunan, known as the Tungting Lake. The Chinese character "Hu" means a lake and "Peh" is north while "Nan" is south. So Hunan is to the south of Hupeh. I was rather surprised to find that the lake could be of such huge size. When our boat sailed over it, I thought I was once more on the open sea! We have many lakes in my native province of Chekiang, and many of them very beautiful of which the West Lake in Hangchow, its capital, is the most famous for its beauty. But the West Lake is but a small pond comparing with the Tungting Lake. The latter is of course not as large as the five lakes separating the United States of America from Canada but to a young man who had never been to a big lake before, it was quite a sight.

The Changsha High School authorities gave me a very warm reception and I was given living quarters, with a Japanese teacher who joined our teaching staff soon after my arrival. We struck up a warm friendship. There was another surprise in store for me. I found the people there talking the same language as those in north China, generally known as the Mandarin, that is the language used by the officials of the country and are known to the western nations as Mandarin.

My native province, though one of the smallest of all the provinces in China, presents the very spectacle of the tower of Babel. People of the same province could not converse with one another! There must be at least a dozen dialects in the province which are as "foreign" as French to the German or the German to the Italian. Yet in this far off inland province they speak a language understood by the northern provinces. I have since traveled all over China. The so-called Mandarin is understood in nine-tenths of the country. Only three provinces and half have dialects which are so different and divergent from one another and from the rest of the country. They are Kwangtung, Fukien, Chekiang and the southern half of Kiangsu and they form the south-eastern part of China. Why this has been so, I have not been able to find out. But it was in these provinces that the contact was first made between China and the western nations, and it was from these provinces where our overseas Chinese migrated to the different countries of the whole world, particular to the South-Sea islands, near east, and America. The erroneous belief that China has a great language difficulty must have been sprung from here. Although these three and half provinces do have several dozens of dialects, yet their written language is exactly the same all over the country. For that I may add that our written language is understood by the Japanese, Koreans as well as parts of the countries bordering on China. When I say that outside of these three provinces and half, the whole nation speak the same language, I do not mean that there are no differences in accents. Some of these accents are quite distinct and noticeable. To one who has traveled extensively in the country, he can always tell where the man with whom he is conversing hails from. I think it is easy to detect whether a particular Englishman is a Londoner, a Scot or an Irish, although he is speaking the same English language.

My coning to Changsha proved to be well timed, for it was at this time the Yale Mission decided to found a new educational institution in China in the very city to which I was bound. From the time when I was a student at Peiyang it was my ambition to do post-graduate work at Yale. The name of Yung Wing, the first Chinese ever to graduate from Yale was the Educational Commissioner in charge of the three groups of Chinese youths sent to America by our government. He was a hero to me. Since my college life was cut short by the Boxer Outbreak, that ambition had never died. In Changsha I met Mr. Seabury the first man sent by the Yale Mission. From him I learned that in order to pass the entrance examination at Yale, I had to have among other requirements, two years of study in Latin. I had sufficient knowledge in French and German to enable me to study at Yale. There and then I started learning Latin. Unfortunately Mr. Seabury was drowned in Kuling with another Yale man, Professor Mann of St. John's University, Shanghai, that summer while vacationing at this famous summer resort. However I continued my Latin study with Mr. Gage, another Yale man sent by the Mission to take Mr. Seabury's place.

My students at the Hunan High School had to begin their English from A. B. C.. Their age ranged from 16 up and some of them were well over 20. It was astonishing to see with what zeal and diligence they applied to their lessons. In less than two years when I had charge of their English studies, they finished all the Eight Readers and acquired quite a working vocabulary to tackle even some of the English classics.

At first we were in the city. Next year a new site was found on an island in the Siang River, which runs from the upper reaches of Hunan to the Tungting Lake passing just outside of the eastern wall of the city. Like all the cities in China it was enclosed in a square wall and our old school site was too congested for the proper growth of our School. The island, though narrow, is fairly long and rather thinly populated. Besides it is blessed with a number of hilly places. The hill which we had selected as our new school site is known as Yolushan, or the Yolu Hill. It is spacious enough to accommodate our school buildings together with athletic field and ball grounds. From the top of the hill it commands an excellent view of the city and the water fronts of the river. My Japanese colleague was quite an athlete. Together with other teachers, we encouraged our boys to take deep interest in athletic activities.

I was happy in my new work in Changsha. The government and

school authorities showed much courtesy to us, considering us as torchbearers of the "new learning movement." And the students were so much devoted to us. I remember once the Governor of the province paid a visit to our school. A table was spread to entertain him. We all thought that he should have the seat of honour, being the highest authority of the province and a mandarin of great eminence, but Governor Chao Er-hsun insisted that the teaching staff should have the seats of honour while he sat at the foot of the table to play the part of a host. This goes to show how teachers in China are so highly honoured.

It had been my practice to visit my homefolks whenever possible. In my student days I could afford only once a year to do it and that during the summer vacations, both because the summer holidays lasted longer and the weather was more conducing to sea travels. During the winter months the sea was rough most of the time. Since my transfer to the inland city of Changsha and in the capacity of a teacher with comparatively munificent income, I could well afford to visit my people twice a year, both during summer and winter vacations. Besides, there was another attraction to wit to have more reunions with my "weaving maid." During these holiday visits, I was also quite busily occupied with my other activities. Believing that athletic activities would help to build up the physique of my people, together with Dr. Chang Po-ling, who later founded the Nankai University in Tientsin, and others who had the same belief, we launched the China National Amateur Athletic Federation in 1905 with headquarters in Shanghai. More will be related in later parts of this book.

One other organization greatly interested me and that was the Y. M. C. A. Movement. Educational institutions are necessary to bring more knowledge to our people, athletic activities to build up their bodies, and religious devotions to promote their spiritual welfare, inasmuch as human beings are born with these three great attributes: the Mind, the Body, and the Soul. I do not belittle the efforts made separately along these three lines, but as the Mind, the Body, and the Soul together make up the Man, efforts made jointly by one organization ought to bring about the best results. Hence the work of the Y. M. C. A. Movement had caught my deep attention and enthusiasm. I threw my whole strength into its activities accordingly.

The type of men sent out to China by the International Committee of Y. M. C. A.'s was of such a high caliber and devotion that won the immediate response of our young men. The work of the Y. M. C. A. spread throughout the country in a way that was really astonishing. In Mr. Fletcher S. Brockman, who was appointed as the General Secretary of the Y. M. C. A.'s in China, you will understand the reason for its phenomenal growth. He was not only well-educated, deeply religious and well-built, he took on a statesmanlike view of any problem that was brought to him. He and I had had many heart-to-heart talks over the best means to increase educational facilities in the country, to bring greater joy to the families, to raise the living standard of the people, and to have a united and strong China. It was during one of our talks in the spring of 1905 that finally led me one step nearer to my goal of a full college education in America.

At the turn of the present century the desire to get a modern education spread like wild fire among the youths of China. The centuries-old system of imperial examinations had been just abolished. The lack of such modern educational institutions at home, coupled with the dazzling success of the Japanese after their war with Russia, led our youths to turn their attention to Japan for the acquisition of such knowledge. Two other factors contributed to the great exodus of our students to Japan. One was and still is the close similarity between the Japanese written language and ours. It takes less time for our students to acquire a working knowledge of the Japanese language for the pursuit of education there. The other was and also still is that, the two countries being neighbours, the cost of traveling to and fro is very much less. By 1905 it was estimated that over twenty thousand of our youths were in Japan of which over ten thousand in Tokyo alone. An opportunity to open a Chinese Young Men's Christian Association in Tokyo naturally presented itself to a farseeing man like Mr. Brockman. He had already sent Mr. J. M. Clinton to Tokyo for a preliminary survey of the situation and to make tentative arrangements with the Japanese Y. M. C. A. leaders for co-operation and was now looking for a Chinese leader to direct the work and his choice fell on me. Although I had been connected with the Y. M. C. A. work for nearly ten years, I was never a paid secretary of the organization and I knew the paid secretary was key to the organization.

We had several long talks over this proposition. I told him very frankly that since I left Peiyang University my one aim was to get a college education in America and nothing would or could divert me from the realization of that aim. With that in view I had been saving every cent I could spare during the last three years and the job of teaching at the Hunan High School gave me a good salary and I was happy at it. I reckoned that at the rate my savings were being accumulated, I could proceed to American by the fall of 1907. Mr. Brockman was most sympathetic with my aspirations and promised me that he would find ways and means to enable me to fulfill my aim. As I was about due to return to Changsha, our conversations ended there, not realizing then that before my spring terms at the Hunan High School was over, Mr. Brockman had a definite plan worked out and urged me to accept the call to proceed to Tokyo to work among the thousands of Chinese youths who were bound to be the future leaders of China.

His plan was that he would secure the promise of two American business men to undertake my tuition and board expenses during my education in America to compensate my loss between the amount of salary I was then receiving and what I would get as a Y. M. C. A. Secretary (for Y. M. C. A. secretaries would only get a living wage) and that I could leave my work in Tokyo before the fall of 1907, so as not to upset the plan I had originally made. In his letter he informed that these two American business men were touring in the Far East and asked me whether I could have a visit with them in Shanghai. Accordingly I asked for two weeks of leave of absence from my school and went to Shanghai.

The two business men tuned out to be Mr. Smith B. Young and Mr. Robert S. Holmes of Lansing, Michigan. They were staunch supporters of the Y. M. C. A. work, both locally and nationally, and the prospect of extending their support internationally appealed to them but they wanted to meet this young upstart to make sure that their investment would bear fruit. At our subsequent meetings, they were as much pleased with me as I was with them. So detailed arrangements were made there and then to the great delight of Mr. Brockman. I was to return to Changsha to finish my term's work at the school and then to proceed to Tokyo in my new capacity of a Y. M. C. A. Secretary.

Hitherto I had been handling boys of the teen-age, although quite a number had passed it, especially at the Hunan High School. The people in Hunan were rather behind in modern education. Now my work in Tokyo brought me in touch with young men fully grown-up, and some of them were much older than I. They came from practically all over China, except a few of the provinces way in the interior. Their tasks also differed very much from what were before the boys at the schools at home, where their teachers had mapped out their lessons for them. Here in Tokyo they were in a foreign country. They must first of all pick up enough of the language as to enable them to understand what their Japanese teachers were lecturing on. They had to decide what lines of education they wanted to take up and what deficiencies they had to make up. Some of them who wanted to study engineering, for instance, found themselves woefully behind in mathematics, while others did not have even the elementary knowledge of chemistry and physics and yet they would like to take up courses in science.

After a careful study of the situation it was felt that the first service the Y. M. C. A. could render would be to organize classes to meet these needs. Special teachers were engaged for these classes. Some were recruited locally but a large number had to be brought over from China. They were not only teachers but also acted as consultants as well. In a very short time our day and evening classes became very popular. We borrowed classrooms from the Japanese Y. M. C. A. and they were filled day and night at such hours when these rooms were not occupied.

Another popular program was to give public lectures on current topics delivered by men of eminence in the various walks of life, among whom I would like to mention Count Okuma (later Marquis), Dr. John R. Mott, Mr. Sherwood Eddy, Dr. Robert Fitch, and a host of others. The Japanese Y. M. C. A. Auditorium could easily seat a thousand people and it was quite often fully filled up. Sometimes we had even to hold overflow meetings.

As these young men were away from their homes, naturally they felt rather homesick at times. So occasionally we had social parties for them with Chinese musical programs.

The central thought of our work is naturally that of religion but it is not in the form of church activities. Not only we are interdenominational, not favouring any particular denomination of the Christian faith, but we also do not propose to proselytize our members to believe in any particular religion. Being a Christian organization we wish to permeate our work with the spirit of Christ who has taught us that God is Love, and it is for us to love Him with all our mind, with all our heart, with all our soul and with all our strength and to love our neighbour as ourselves. Naturally, we had Bible classes for those who wanted to know about Christianity, but we had also classes for the study of comparative religions.

Our work was well received by the Chinese student body, so much so that we had to organize a branch Y. M. C. A. near the Waseda University which was well attended by the large number of students studying at that University. Due to lack of funds we did not attempt to have another branch at Kyoto or Osaka. There were sufficient numbers of Chinese students in these cities to warrant the organization of such a branch.

It was in Tokyo where I came in contact with Dr. Sun Yat-sen, the Father of our Republic. He was then a political refugee in Japan, being hunted by the Chinese government for his revolutionary activities to overthrow the much hated alien Manchu dynasty. I had heard a great deal about his activities and was much in sympathy with his views. While teaching at the Anglo-Chinese College in Tientsin, I had made up my mind to discard my queue and to work for a free, united and strong China. After several visits with him and being convinced of his sincerity and ability to bring about a successful revolution, I decided to join his political party, the Tung Meng Hui, or Political Alliance, which was naturally a secret organization. He himself administered the oath to me when I signed up to join the Revolution. From this time on I had an additional aspiration, to wit, that after I got a full college education in America, I was to throw myself heart and soul into the revolutionary movement when I returned to my homeland.

Before I set sail for America in the early summer of 1907, I paid a flying visit to Shanghai, both to see my homefolks and to make a personal report to Mr. Brockman on my stewardship of the Y. M. C. A. work in Tokyo. My parents and my wife together with our two little girls came up from Ningpo to have this family reunion. My second daughter was still in her mother's arms. I could see that my father was both happy and sad. He was much gratified that my aspiration to study abroad for a full college education was about to be realized. It was he who first guided me towards getting a modern education by urging me to try the examination held by the Peiyang University authorities in Shanghai. And he was proud of my record of success, both as a teacher and a Y. M. C. A. Secretary. Somehow he had an admonition that he would never see me again in person after this visit, as eventually it proved to be. He passed away in 1911 while I was still studying for my Master's degree at Yale. I did not realize that I would not see my second daughter either, for she also died soon after I reached America.

Mr. Brockman was quite satisfied with my work in Tokyo. We had collected a very strong secretarial staff and had secured Mr. H. H. Kung to take my place as the General Secretary. Mr. Kung is the 75th lineal descendant of Confucius and an ardent Christian worker. He had graduated from Oberlin and took postgraduate course at Yale. He was one of the two boys made famous by a book written by their American teacher, entitled: Two Sons of Cathay. I may add that the other "Son of Cathay," Mr. H. J. Fei, later became the General Secretary of our Peking Y. M. C. A..

After bidding farewell to my homefolks and a host of friends, I returned to Tokyo. Then I sailed for the land of my dreams in the company of Mr. John F. Williams, a very dear friend and a colleague of our Y. M. C. A. work in Tokyo. He was the Vice-President of the Nanking University, temporarily loaned to our Y. M. C. A. work in Tokyo, and was returning to America on furlough together with his wife and family, so I was most fortunate to start out on my first long voyage in the company of a charming American family.

Chapter 4

Glimpses of American Life

My original plan was to go direct to Yale, but as my two friends who promised to help me financially during my education in America happened to live in Lansing, Michigan, and at the advice of my good friend, Fletcher Brockman, I agreed to enroll for the first year at the University of Michigan at Ann Arbor. The latter had made arrangement with Mr. Lincoln E. Buell, who was then the General Secretary of the Y. M. C. A. in the State of Michigan, to take me in as his boarder. I have never regretted of this new arrangement, for it had given me an opportunity to study the life of an American family at close hand, for I was taken in almost as a member of the family. Moreover, by attending first a university founded and supported by a State and later an endowment university, I was enabled to notice the considerable differences between them both in respect of equipment and student life.

I believe the Buell's represent a typical American family, happy and congenial. They had a home large enough to hold the three generations under one roof, with over ten acres of land surrounding it. Mr. Buell was then a widower, having lost his wife several years ago, leaving his four sons in the care of his sister, Miss Flora Buell. He was most of the time attending his duties in Detroit but frequently came home to visit with his homefolks. Mother Buell was younger than my own grandmother when I was a little boy but slightly older than my mother. Besides Flora, Mr. Buell had two other sisters, Jeanette and Bertha, and a brother Frank. The four sons ranged between thirteen and seven. Miss Bertha Buell, being the youngest sister, was then at the Teacher's College in Ypsilanti, just halfway between Ann Arbor and Detroit. She came home during the weekends. In this happy home I stayed nearly a year. I felt I was in my own home in Ningpo.

The first thing that struck me was the way the boys were taught early to take on some kind of work besides their studies, with due compensation for their work. Each boy opened an account with his father which registered his earnings day by day. Josiah was then old enough to do a man's work side by side with his uncle Frank. He was to help looking after the horses and cows, scrubbing them, drove the wagon, and did the marketing. Everett and Bruce were still too young to do any heavy work, but they distributed the morning milk on their bicycles. Roy was only seven but he had his duties, to help feeding the large number of chickens kept at the farm, and to do odds and ends as directed by his aunt Flora. The boys could take off time in their daily duties and naturally would lose their due compensations. I am absolutely convinced that free labour with due compensations gets much better result than slave labour, for I seldom found these boys not doing their daily chores.

When I first arrived at the family, I did not realize that they would start their work so early in the morning. I went down to the dining room next morning at about 7 o'clock and hoped I would not be too early. To my great surprise, they had finished their breakfast long ago. The young maid brought me mine and I ate alone. So the next morning I arrived at the dining room at six o'clock when the sun was just peeping out in the east. Behold, I was late again! The breakfast was already over but I could see that it was just finished as the maid was clearing the table. So on the following morning I set my alarm clock to wake me up at five and had to turn the light on for my bath and toilet. To my great delight I was able to join the family at breakfast for the first time. From then on I was always with them. Instead of studying in the evenings, I would prepare my lessons after breakfast before riding up to the University to attend my classes. The Buell house was then just outside of the city limit and is about three miles from the University Campus.

There had been few Chinese to graduate from Michigan up to my time. Of these Dr. Mary Stone and Dr. Ida Kahn became very prominent in their medical work on their return to China. They were natives of the province of Kiangsi, just to the east of the province of Hunan. Receiving their early education at a mission school in China, their teacher sent them to Michigan for their medical course. An interesting story had been told about Mary Stone. Chinese names are often

Chapter 4 Glimpses of American Life

very difficult to pronounce. All Chinese characters are monosyllable, when a mistake is made in pronouncing them, it is impossible to tell to whom it is referred. Miss Mary Stone's Chinese surname is SHIH, which gave the American professors a good deal of difficulty in pronouncing it correctly but it means a stone. So after a year or so, Miss Stone decided to use the English translation of her surname. One morning her professor was calling her name. Getting no response, he thought he was not pronouncing it correctly, so tried several ways to the best of his ability. Finally Miss Stone got on her feet and blushing profusely said, "Please, Sir, I have changed my name to Stone." Thinking that the young lady had been recently married, the Professor replied most cordially, "Hearty congratulations, Mrs. Stone," to the great merriment of the whole class.

When I enrolled in Michigan in 1907, there were only six other Chinese students in Ann Arbor, one in the Graduate School, two in College, one in the Engineering School, and two in the High School. The one in the Graduate School eventually won his Ph. D. degree and became a well-known figure in diplomatic circles in London. Dr. W. C. Chen was for many years a member of our Embassy in London, worked his way to become its First Secretary and Chancellor and was Chargés d'Affaires several times. One of the two boys in the High School entered the Law School of the University after graduating from the High School with high honours. Mr. Albino Z. SyCip did not sound like a Chinese. People thought he was a Filipino, but he is 100% (per cent) Chinese, although born in Manila. SyCip was really his father's name, Sy being the surname and Cip his given name. It has been the custom of our overseas Chinese to give the father's surname and name as the surname of his children.

There was also an interesting anecdote told on SyCip. When he entered the Ann Arbor High School, his English was rather deficient. One day as he was ordering his meal, the waiter asked him whether he would like to have a beefsteak, either rare, medium or well-done. As he was averse to having a beefsteak for his meal and thinking that "well-done" was another dish he could have and it was a high-sounding one, he ordered "well-done." To his dismay what the waiter did bring to him was still a beefsteak although quite well-done. He indignantly pointed out to the waiter that he did not order beefsteak but a well-done, in quite a loud tone. When the other patrons at the Café

39

turned their eyes on him, he felt so humiliated that he walked out of the Café without his meal. And yet at his graduation from the High School, he was given a citation on the excellence of his English! This goes to show how well a Chinese student could master any subject when he sets his mind on it. Mr. SyCip has since become a distinguished banker in Manila, having been for many years President and General Manager of the China Banking Corporation, the leading Chinese bank in the Philippines.

The number of Chinese students at the university has been much increased since then. When I visited Ann Arbor in 1948, I was told there were more than four hundred of them enrolled that year. The growth in number was largely caused by a larger number of Chinese youths seeking western education in America. Two other factors contributed to the larger proportion of increase in Michigan as compared with endowment universities. The first is that a state university being heavily subsidized by the state could afford to charge much lower tuitions. State born citizens were only charged a nominal tuition while that charged on an alien is but slightly larger. Moreover, the cost of living in Ann Arbor is much lower than in big cities, such as New York, Chicago or Boston. As most of our students who go abroad to study are private ones, less cost in tuition and board, while the standard of education is just as high and good as the endowment universities, is a natural attraction to them.

Another important factor in drawing our students to Michigan University is the friendly interest of the people in Ann Arbor in the foreign students. There is no aloofness on the part of the town people towards the students, popularly known as "the town and the gown." In the big cities the town people and the student bodies are separate entities. The only intercourse between them is just trade. In Ann Arbor, however, most of the students, whether native or alien, take rooms and often board with the families living there. Soon they struck up deep and lasting friendships between them. This particularly appeals to our Chinese students who love to have home atmosphere surrounding them.

America has always been known as the land of opportunities. Before I went there I had read about the immigrants from the countries of the old world how by dint of hard work, most of them succeeded to maintain a higher standard of living than their folks at

Chapter 4 Glimpses of American Life

home, because opportunities were open to them to make use of their abilities and talents which were denied them in their homelands. I would not have dared to leave my own country for a full college education in a foreign country with no financial support either from my father or from my government but for the knowledge I had that I would get opportunities to pay my way. The first opportunity came in the form of financial backing from two American businessmen whom I had never met before. They assured me of meeting my tuition and board so long as I should make good in my studies. In this I had no misgivings. But the meager savings I had been able to accumulate while teaching in Tientsin and Changsha, would not carry me very far after meeting my outfit and traveling expenses. However, other opportunities came and knocked at my door from unexpected and unsolicited quarters.

Shortly after I was admitted to Michigan University, I was startled one bright morning to receive a message from President Angell to go to his office at an appointed time. I wondered whether I had violated any of the school rules, calling for disciplinary admonishing. I went there as ordered and when the President received me as if I were his favourite son, my heart was at once set at ease. After preliminary greetings and telling me how happy he was to see me in the University, for he was once America's Minister at Peking. He explained to me that a court in Chicago was trying a Chinese murder case and was looking for a Chinese student to help the court in translating certain evidence into English, that I would have all my traveling and hotel expenses paid for, and that he would give me leave of absence so as not to affect my class attendance. He asked me whether I would be willing to undertake the trip, and whether I had any request to make. Here now was an opportunity to visit Chicago, one of the great cities of America, without any expenses to myself, and of course I took it with stretched hands so to speak, but I was diplomatic enough not to show too much eagerness to grasp it. In my turn I explained to Dr. Angell that I was new in the country and that my knowledge in legal matters might be insufficient in the proper discharge of my duties. I wondered whether I could have another Chinese student to go with me so as to give me both company and assistance. He readily agreed to this request and I named W. C. Chen, the one who was taking a post graduate course at the University. It would not require much imagination to see how happy a couple of Chinese students could be to receive their first commission to do some work for Uncle Sam, as we boarded the train to take us to Chicago.

We were met at the Chicago station by a representative from the court and taken to a nice hotel. The documents to be translated into English were turned over to us and we were asked how long it would take us to complete the translation. We estimated that it would take from three to four days. As a matter of fact we concluded our work in less than three days. The trial was to take place on the fifth day after our arrival, so Mr. Chen and I had two full days for sight-seeing. On the day of trial we were asked to attend the court so as to be on hand. During the trial, questions were asked both by prosecuting attorney and the defence lawyer, to which the accused, who was about 45 years of age, gave due replies. His English was rather limited, so most of the answers were given in the Cantonese dialect. There was a court interpreter, also a Cantonese but his knowledge of English was only slightly better. Sensing that I could do the interpreting more satisfactorily, as I happened to know the Cantonese dialect as well, I offered my services to the court. The trial lasted the whole day and judgement was reserved for the next day when he was found "not guilty" by the jury and was acquitted. We were thanked by the Judge for our work and decided to return to Ann Arbor on the following day. We thought that was the end of our mission. But another surprise was in store for us. On return to our hotel after doing some more sight-seeing we found the same representative from the court awaiting us with a cheque for $350 for each of us. We were told that the Court considered us as experts and that we were each entitled to receive $50 per day as our compensation! I must own up that I had never made so much money per day up to that time, or even when I was a Minister of State in our own government for that matter.

Mr. Chen and I had quite a discussion that evening as to how best to commemorate our work for Uncle Sam. I cannot recall now what he bought, but I bought a Waltham watch at the Montgomery for $75. What extravagance! Just imagine that a poor student from overseas should keep a watch of that value. I did not have the nerve to use it openly but I took good care of it and keep it as a treasure. After I won my Phi Beta Kappa key at Yale three years later, I put the watch and the key in my treasury box, only to be fondled in privacy. One day when I was attending a Y. M. C. A. conference at Northfield, I met a Mrs. Lyons, who wanted to see my key. Her husband was also a Yale graduate who had won the key. So I took my treasury box to have the key inspected and incidentally she saw the watch also. I believe that a woman has what is known as the sixth sense. Without any explanation whatever, she concluded that I needed a chain to string the watch and key together for everyday use. Either I did not want to spend any more money to buy the chain or I did not have the nerve to display the honours I had won, she made a mental reservation to present me with a chain. Several weeks later I received a chain from her after she returned to her home on the Pacific coast together with a letter explaining that the chain had been used by Mr. Lyons during his life time and wanted me to keep it as a souvenir in his memory. To this day, the watch, the key and the chain constitute the best treasure in my possession, not so much for their intrinsic values but for their spiritual worth.

There is another angle of the American life which I believe should be promoted in every country, and that is to create a strong desire to learn and understand the other peoples of the world. It accounts for the large number of the American tourists. Those that can afford the expenses make visits to other countries, but others not in such fortunate circumstances still devise other means to satisfy their desire towards that end. Civic Leagues, Y. M. C. A's church organizations and other Associations constantly invite speakers of different nationalities to address them, inevitably paying their traveling expenses and often giving them an honorarium as well, ranging from twenty to a hundred dollars and sometimes even larger sums. A comparatively unknown person like me, when I was only a student, had received many such invitations. In some meetings as many as several hundred would be present, while in others less than hundred. Whether the audience be large or small, that eagerness to know and learn is always clearly manifested.

From time immemorial there have been wars among the different peoples of the world and some of the wars have proved to be most destructive in life and property. Many great sages, philosophers and religious teachers have denounced war, yet the present world is still gripped by wars and the fears of wars. There are many causes which have brought about wars. Personal ambitions of powerful leaders, whether known as Chiefs, Kings, Caesars, Emperors and what not, economic differences between the peoples, popularly dubbed as "the have's" and the "have-not's," religious emotions, or opposite ideological tenets contribute towards the making of wars. I am fully convinced that the greatest cause of all is the ignorant prejudices of one nation against another, so the most effective means to promote world peace is to encourage the nations of the world to know and understand one another. World organizations like the Rotary Clubs are decidedly making concrete contributions towards world peace by promoting international understanding and good-will.

Americans are noted for their generosity and quick response to any appeal for a good cause. An instance may be cited of a meeting at the White House in the spring of 1908 in which I participated. The purpose of the meeting was to make appeals for help towards the building up of the work of the Young Men's Christian Associations throughout the world. President Theodore Roosevelt kindly gave permission to have the meeting held at the White House to which quite a large number of leading American business men were invited. The policy of the Association has always been that local units must find the necessary funds to finance their work from the communities in which they are located but appeals for the erection of buildings and for equipments could be made in other countries. Dr. John R. Mott was then the General Secretary of the International Committee of the entire Y. M. C. A. Movement. Under his able leadership, assisted by the General Secretaries of the various National Committees, the whole campaign for the solicitation of funds was planned and successfully carried out. Mr. Fletcher S. Brockman, the General Secretary of the Chinese National Committee was present to look after the China end.

Although the Y. M. C. A. Movement in China was only then a little more than a decade old, its growth was quite spectacular. In most of the larger cities it had struck its root. Four of these cities, Peking, Shanghai, Hankow and Canton, were considered strong enough to have a well-equipped Y. M. C. A. building, and their total cost would be about a million U. S. dollars. I was selected to be the spokesman for China. After obtaining leave of absence from the Michigan University authorities, I set out for Washington and to meet Dr. Mott

Chapter 4 Glimpses of American Life

and Mr. Brockman for my briefing. After acquainting me with the purpose of the meeting, its composition, and the amount of money to be raised for China, I was told to make a speech for eight minutes only, as there were speakers for other countries on the agenda. To say that I was surprised to have this rare honour to address such a distinguished audience in the presence of the American President, would be too mild a statement. I was really quite frightened over my responsibility. What, if I should fail in my appeal!

I wrote and re-wrote my speech and had the final version committed to memory after timing it with my Waltham watch to see that I did not use more than eight minutes. I was sitting between Dr. Mott and Mr. Brockman in the audience before my turn to go to the platform to deliver my speech. They were there, I believe, to give me moral support, although I was unaware of it at the time. When my turn came, all my fear and trepidation were gone. I felt like a warrior going out to battle. Within the prescribed time I made my speech, at the end of which I was given a rousing applause, loud and long. The Chairman of the meeting, Commissioner McDowell of the District of Columbia, was the first man to grip my hand and warmly congratulated me, and told me it was a most inspirational address. I returned to my seat. Both Dr. Mott and Mr. Brockman treated me like a conquering hero coming home. Then I saw slips of paper were being sent up by the ushers from the audience to the Chairman who began adding up the amount of contributions towards our four buildings. Finally, he rose from the Chair, with his face beaming, and announced that up to that moment a total of one million and eighty thousand dollars had been pledged to the support of our China work. I closed my eyes and thanked the Lord for the inspiration He gave me. The generosity and quick response of the American people was then and there deeply impressed upon my mind and strongly felt in my heart.

American love for freedom and independence is another phase of their life that highly impresses me, for I myself come from a people who consider freedom and independence dearer than even life itself. We Chinese are more patient and could endure more and longer suffering, but sometimes I believe we are too patient. My own participation in our revolution of 1911 was greatly influenced by my study of the American Revolutionary War for independence. As I traveled about in the United States, an opportunity given to few students of limited means, I was impressed with that spirit not only by statues and war memorials, such as the Statue of Liberty at the entrance of the New York harbour or the Independence Hall in Philadelphia with the Liberty Bell, but also by what I saw in their daily life. Among my fellow students, both at Michigan and Yale, there were many who worked their way through college and some of them had quite wealthy parents. The example set by the Buell boys in getting to work in their very young age would give them the stamina to be independent should any calamity fall on their parent, the bread-winner of the family. In this case nothing happened to Mr. Buell who lived to a ripe old age, taking good care of his children, but generally it is a wise practice to teach children to be able to stand on their own feet if ever such a situation should arise.

The Americans are noted for their ability to organize whether on a grand or small scale and irrespective of the purpose of the organization or its duration. They just love to be banded together. For trivial purposes and for short durations, such as picnic parties or excursion trips, or for important causes, like the Red Cross Societies, Christian Missions, educational institutions and many others, or for business enterprises, or for political purposes, the Americans would put their heart and soul into them, and they start early in their lives to get into the habit of getting organized. Take for instance the collage fraternities. They are there by the dozens. The average college boy would remain in college only for four years. Some of the fraternities would begin to tap in new members in their sophomore year while others would not admit them until their senior year. So the association of a fraternity member with the other brothers of the organization is of very short duration, yet most of the fraternities are well organized and financed. Some have created permanent homes for their organizations. The reason is that fraternities teach them how to organize. Problems, like the choice of leadership, the recruiting of new members, the financing of the organization, etc., would have to be tackled early in their lives, and the experiences gained thereby are worth as much to them as the knowledge they get from the classrooms in their afterlives. American leadership in the present worldwide organizations has to be traced to what the present leaders have learned in their college days.

Chapter 5

Chinese Students' Activities

At the time when I was a student at the Michigan University, I believe there were less than a thousand Chinese students in the United States, not counting those who were born in America of our overseas Chinese parentage. They were widely scattered from the Pacific coast to the Atlantic but the bulk of them were concentrated along the Atlantic coast as far west as Chicago. Some of these students were there at the expense of our government, whether national, provincial or local, but the majority of them were private students. The wealthier families usually sent their children to Yale, Harvard, Princeton, Columbia, or Cornell where the expenses were much higher. Still there were some students of limited means among them who preferred these universities for one reason or another.

In order to promote better acquaintance and to work for their common welfare an organization was already in existence by the time I went to Michigan. It was known as the Chinese Students' Alliance and was well organized. An annual conference was held in some locality nearest to the bulk of the Chinese students lasting for four or five days, at which the usual program of a conference was carried out. There were addresses from distinguished persons who took an interest in our students, discussions groups on various topics facing our student life, and social gatherings. Often, picnic parties were arranged to visit the beauty spots of the city where the conference was being held. There was usually a big dinner party to which Chinese diplomatic representatives, officials of the city government and other distinguished guests were invited. The highlight of the conference is the election of officers, particularly the President, of the organization, for the ensuing year. The delegations from the various universities would press for the election of their "favourite son" to be chosen to head the movement. This election took place usually towards the end of the conference. Before the election meeting was held, it would be plain to any observer that the place was highly charged with an election atmosphere. Groups of students would meet behind closed doors and emissaries would once a while sally forth to negotiate with other groups. The election campaign was on. It was a good lesson to them on their return home how to run a democratic government.

The first conference I attended was held at Hartford, Connecticut, on the campus of a well known college in the late summer of 1908. It was a well-chosen place for the meeting. The New England states had early contacts with China and with Chinese students. American business men, largely drawn from these states, were among the first settlers in Canton and they kept contact with their home bases by the then well-know Flying Clippers, ships which sailed from Boston to the Far East.

The three groups of our boys sent by our government under the guidance of Yung Wing were also brought to these states in the early seventies of the last century. The New Englanders have evinced warm friendships for our people and as warmly reciprocated by us.

I was a new-comer so to speak having only studied at Michigan for one year, but I participated in all the activities of the conference. Being older in age than most of them and having had experience in the handling of affairs and men, I had apparently made favorable impressions in their minds. Without any solicitation on my part my name was put up as one of the candidates for the President of the organization. I thought I would have little chances in getting elected. To my great surprise when the votes were counted I received more than majority and was declared elected by the Chairman of the conference. Fortunately, I had decided to enroll at Yale and was already admitted as sophomore but with the understanding that I would be advanced to the senior class in the fall of 1909, if I could take four extra units to be so qualified. To this I readily agreed so as to shorten my stay in America. As all the other officers to be associated with me were studying in nearby universities, I found I could contact them without much loss of time. I succeeded in finding time to give proper attention both to the administration of our organization and to my studies. Both seemed to be satisfied with my work, for I was chosen at the next conference to be the Editor of our magazine, known as the Chinese Students' Monthly and admitted to the senior class in 1909.

In that same year another organization to be known as the Chinese Students' Christian Association came into existence. It was organized by those of the Chinese students who believed in the Christian religion and the object was to bring Christianity to the attention of other students by holding Bible Classes for them and by inducing them to attend Church Services. I was chosen as its first General Secretary and the work required quite frequent and extensive traveling throughout the States. It gave me unique opportunities to visit colleges and universities where Chinese students were in attendance. I did cover quite a wide area as time permitted. Wherever I could, I had meetings held to call the attention of our students to the study of Christian religion and to organize local chapters with Christian students, both Chinese and American, as the nucleus.

During my visitations I found most of our students were doing well in their studies. Their ex-curriculum activities were, however, rather limited. Few of them had joined the fraternities, and still fewer took parts in athletics and ball games. They concentrated their full attention to the absorption of knowledge. Consequently their ratings were quite high and a number of them had won the much coveted Phi Beta Kappa keys. Some had developed much [many] literary and forensic powers, having won positions in the editing of their college dailies or in the open oratorical contests. It is to be noted that they won these honours in a language that is foreign to them.

In most of the colleges and universities I visited, I found Chinese Students' Clubs well organized, carrying on quite actively social functions and club life. Once a while they would even enter into contacts with other clubs in the form of oratorical contests or debates. I took part in one of such inter-club occasions. There was arranged a debate between Chinese students of Pennsylvania and Yale. The subject of the debate was: Resolved that the Lunar Calendar is more useful to China than the Solar. Pennsylvania Chinese Students' Club was to defend the resolution with the Yale Club opposing it. Judges were selected and accepted by both clubs.

The Lunar Calendar has been used in China throughout the centuries. The beauty of it is that the Moon is always full by the middle of each month, whereas by the Solar Calendar the full moon is seldom seen by the middle of each month, and may fall on any day, hence special markings have to be made to indicate when the full moon is to be expected. In almost all the western countries, however, the Solar Calendar has been followed. Our people have called the Solar Calendar as the "Western Calendar" and the Lunar as "Chinese Calendar." In view of the adoption of the Solar Calendar as the standard calendar for China after the establishment of the Republic of China in 1911, the debate between the two Chinese Students' Clubs portended what was soon to happen.

I was chosen Leader of our team. We discussed the best ways to demonstrate that the Solar Calendar is more useful to our people than the Lunar. We found the key to the question by asking ourselves why our forefathers while adopting the lunar calendar should have instituted also the twenty-four "seasonal changes" in each year whether the year has the ordinary twelve months or thirteen months during the leap years. By studying the past ten years according to the solar calendar, it is found there are eight cardinal "seasonal changes," namely the beginning and ending of each of the four seasons, spring, summer, autumn and winter. They are known as Li-ch'un (立春), Li-hsia (立夏), Li-ch'iu (立秋) and Li-tung (立冬), with the letter "Li" (立) connotating the beginning; and Ch'un-fen (春分), Hsia-chih (夏至), Ch'iu-fen (秋分) and Tung-chih (冬至), with the letters "fen" (分) and "chih" (至) both meaning the ending. The other sixteen "seasonal changes" merely indicate the gradual changes taking place between the four cardinal seasons. So our forefathers were indeed most intelligent in adopting the lunar calendar together with the twenty-four "seasonal changes" as a guide to our people, so that we have a full moon to look at by the middle of each month and yet have the "seasonal changes" to indicate the best times to sow and reap. The beginning of each of the four seasons falls in the first week of February, May, August and November, while the ending falls in the last week of March, June, September and December of each solar calendar year. Summer always ends on the 22nd of June and winter on the 22nd of December, generally known as the summer solstice and the winter solstice.

We anticipated that our opponents would dwell upon the importance of our farmers in the life of our people. It was estimated then, and I believe it is still true now, that eighty-five per centum of our people are agrarian. They would argue that the lunar calendar has been in use in China from time immemorial and a change to the solar

Chapter 5 Chinese Students' Activities

calendar or system would upset the farmers thereby inflicting harmful effects upon the whole people. The leader of our opposing team began his oration exactly on the line we anticipated. When my turn came, I went along his line almost agreeing to every word he said but at the psychological moment I showed to my audience, including the judges of course, that our farmers have always followed the twenty-four "seasonal changes" to guide them in their labour, as to the best time to sow certain crops, and the "seasonal changes" follow the Sun and not the Moon. I then unfolded the calendars for the past ten years, that is, between 1899 and 1908, how the twenty-four "seasonal changes" fall exactly on the months according to the solar calendar but varied every year by the lunar calendar. The argument was so vivid and forceful that there was hardly any leg for our opponents to stand upon. After the usual routine of debates with the presentation of the question by each of the two teammates, followed with rebuttals of the leaders, the judges retired to deliberate on their findings. Within a few minutes they re-appeared and we knew we had won. Our team was awarded a silver cup donated by our diplomatic representative in Washington.

When the three groups of Chinese students were sent to America in the early seventies of the last century, they were all young boys ranging between twelve and sixteen years of age. Being placed at the well-known Prep Schools in the New England States, they took part in all the activities of the American boys. Baseball was practically unknown in China but some of our boys played the game well. As they advanced their studies and were admitted to colleges, they took active parts in all social and athletic events. Some had won distinctions. The coxswain of the Yale crew who won the annual boat-race from Harvard was one of them, Mr. Chung Mun-yew. He was light in weight but had good knowledge of and a sharp eye for the running current of the river.

For about two decades there were hardly any large number of Chinese students in America. On the turn of the present-century, however, the number began to increase. With the return of the so-called Boxer Indemnity by the American government to China, followed by the other western countries which had exacted the Indemnity from China after the Boxer Outbreak, fund was made available to renew the sending of Chinese students to American colleges. Besides, there was growing among our Chinese people a sentiment that western education was a necessary part in the training of our youths to tackle the reform movement for the country. The students who went to America at this period were older in age and were able to enter the various educational institutions of the college grade. They did good work in their studies but, with very few exceptions, hardly took any active part in the social and athletic events.

The Tsing Hua College, later known as Tsing Hua University, was founded in Peking soon after the American Indemnity Fund was made available. After careful screening a large number of its students were sent to America to take up undergraduate studies. Later as the standard of education began to be built up, the college authorities decided to send only its own graduates for post-graduate work. Moreover, other institutions either founded by the government like the Peiyang and Nanyang Universities, or by missionary societies, like the St. Johns, Yenching, Linnan and others, had more and more of their graduate students seeking further education abroad. Consequently, the life of our students in America in the last two or three decades differed very much from those of the earlier periods. They took more active parts in research work and hardly participated in the frivolities of the undergraduate students.

Chapter 6

The 1911 Revolution

1911 was a sad year for me personally. Due to strenuous efforts to graduate with the class of 1910, coupled with duties and responsibilities put upon me as President of the Chinese Students' alliance in 1908, Editor of Chinese Students' Monthly and General Secretary of the Chinese Students' Christian Association the following year, I was not as robust and strong as I used to be. During the first few months of my postgraduate work at Yale, there were signs of that dreaded disease of tuberculosis. So I gave up all my ex-curriculum activities and confined myself to my studies only. By the spring of 1911 I was alarmed by my loss in weight and appetite and the unusual sweating especially at night even in the cold months. I went to consult a doctor who strongly advised me to give up even my studies and take a complete rest. Then in March I received word from home that my beloved father had just passed away. It was he who guided me in the path I had taken from the time I entered the Peiyang University in 1895 until I left China for America in 1907. He gave me the inspiration and encouragement to obtain a full western education and I felt over his death so badly that my health became rather alarming to my doctor. After several prayerful days, I decided to follow his advice and quitted Yale, hoping to return there after my health was fully recovered. I did not realize then that my college days were over then and forever.

I was advised to go to Switzerland and get a rest cure in Davos Platz. This was my first visit to that land of great beauties. I have always been frilled [sic] by beautiful mountain sceneries and bodies of water, whether lakes, rivers or oceans, and Switzerland is full of such beauties. The climate there is simply superb. In less than three months I was completely restored in health and was allowed to continue my journey homeward, through the Suez Canal, reaching Shanghai by the fall of that year. That was also my first trip around the world, without realizing that there was a Hand much greater than human hands in guiding the destiny of every human being. In fact I was being called back to China to take an active part in the great revolution which rocked the Chinese nation from its very foundation. The Revolution of 1911 was not only a political one for China but also economical as well as social. All these three aspects of the revolution are still in the process of developments which are bound to give this nation of 450,000,000 people an impetus towards a new civilization, politically, economically and socially.

To understand the potentialities of this great revolution, one must look into the long history of China, covering a period of over forty centuries. Before that it was lost in mythology. Authentic history was made possible only after the gradual development of calligraphy, consisting of words or characters which at first were images of the objects to be described, followed with systematic combinations to indicate actions, forms, colours, kinds, and so forth, thereby forming the Chinese literature of approximately 50,000 characters. Confucius was the great master in auditing the well-known Four Books and Five Classics.

By a careful study of this long history, certain fundamental traits of the characteristics of the Chinese people stand out very clearly. The foremost is that this people have strong physical endurance. Hardships, adversities, military defeats and even plagues could not deter them from ever increasing in number. What was the size of the population who first settled in the northwestern corner of China is still unknown. It could not have been more than a few millions, but the race continued to grow in number. At the present moment there is yet no authentic census of our population. The best authorities estimate there are from 375,000,000 to about 500,000,000, hence the popular figure of 450,000,000 as the size of our people. At any rate we constitute about a sixth of the human race and have the largest population among all the nations of the world.

A collateral trait is that the size of our country continues to expand. Starting from a small corner in the northwest it spread to the freshets of the Yellow River during the Chow dynasty, then to the Yellow River basin under the Han dynasty, and continue its progress eastward, northward and southward, until it reached its zenith in the Tang dynasty when Chinese authority was being exercised from Siberia to the South Seas.

Another prominent trait is that the Chinese never applied force for expansion. Naturally, forces were used for our defense. We had to fight the Tartars, the Mongols, the Manchus and other hordes from the north for centuries and centuries. Many times in our history we were overrun by them and twice we had even to accept their rule over us as evidenced by the Yuan and Ts'ing dynasties under the Mongols and the Manchus respectively. And yet in the end we came out victors. Not only we took over our territories but absorbed their people as well. It is our profound belief that it is not force but a moral strength that wins in the end. Herein is to be found the unconquerable power of assimilation.

There is one more trait in our people which I must mention before I start to relate the story of the 1911 revolution. It is our deep-rooted love for freedom. From time immemorial this strong love has shown time and again either by individuals or by the nation as a whole. Innumerable examples of men and women who preferred death to being enslaved either physically or mentally, could be cited from this long history. Our classics are full of statements emphasizing the importance and value of freedom. Mencius, a disciple of Confucius, had it stated in a pithy sentence that no lover of freedom could be allured by profits, effected by high positions, or bent by force. The valiant struggles for freedom by the nation in overthrowing the Mongols and Manchus from the thrones of China are vivid examples of our love for freedom. As a matter of fact our people would not stand the despotism of any monarch even of our own race. Our history abounds in instances of the overthrow of monarchs who sought to rule over the people by exercising despotic powers.

The best illustration of this kind is to be found in our history during the Chin dynasty. The founder of this dynasty was among the most powerful monarchs of the world. Having overcome his six other rivals, who ruled over large sections of China stretching from the north of the Yellow River to the south of the Yangtze River, he unified the whole country and brought it under his supreme control. It was he who built the Great Wall of China, starting from Shan-hai-kwan on the east coast bordering on the Pacific Ocean and running westward to the steppes of the high mountains in northwest China, covering a distance of nearly a thousand miles. The wall was to protect China from the raids of nomadic Tartars and Mongols from the north. In spite of the great powers he exercised, the scholars of his realm would not stop criticizing him for any mistakes he made. This irked him so much that he finally decided to put a permanent stop to it by having all the leading scholars put to death in a wholesale manner. He invited about three thousand of them to a gigantic state dinner, meanwhile had secretly a big grave made ready for them. At a given signal they were hauled off from their banquet, brought to the grave and had them buried alive! Believing that these scholars had their inspiration for freedom from the classical books they studied he also ordered that all these books wherever found should be burnt and thousands upon thousands of volumes of books were thus destroyed.

The exercise of such despotic powers did not awe the people at all. Secretly and steadily they strived to overthrow him at the sacrifice of many lives in their efforts. It is true that he died before the people succeeded in overthrowing him but his successor had to pay the supreme penalty for his despotism. Of the seventeen dynasties recorded in our history, the Chin dynasty is the shortest, having only two Emperors on the throne!

The 1911 Revolution was a fight for freedom on the part of the Chinese people. Ever since the fall of the Ming dynasty in 1644, the Manchus had a firm grip over the country. The Manchu Emperors had shown wise statesmanship in that Chinese laws were applied, Chinese customs respected and Chinese nationals were appointed to practically all the key positions in the government. Nevertheless, the fact that it was an alien rule was repugnant to the Chinese love for freedom. In spite of several attempts to overthrow this alien yoke, at huge sacrifice of life and property, this dynasty had lasted for two and half centuries. The last attempt by the Taipings came very near to success. The rebellion, started in Kwangtung and Kwangsi, had pushed its way beyond the Yangtze River by the middle of last century and would have succeeded in founding a new dynasty with a Chinese Emperor on the throne, had the leaders of the rebellion remained true to their original objective of gaining freedom from an alien rule and by united efforts to establish a government which would bring prosperity to the people. Being intoxicated with their partial success, they degenerated into guerrilla bands, each fighting for powers and lootings. The people under their rule suffered so much that instead of giving aid and help to them, they actually hated these bands, who killed their men, raped their women and looted or burned their properties. On the other hand some able Chinese were appointed by the Manchu court to put down the rebellion, of whom the most prominent was Tseng Kuo-fan. Even westerners living in China, like the American Mr. Ward and the British General Gordon, offered their services to the Manchu Government. The rebellion was finally crushed by the later sixties of last century. But the fire for freedom from an alien rule was still burning strong in the breasts of the patriots, only awaiting for a leader to guide them on the road to success. Such a leader finally emerged in the person of Dr. Sun Yat-sen, the father of the Republic of China.

Dr. Sun was born in Heung-shan now known as Chung-shan which was his popular name known to the Chinese people. He was partly educated in Hong Kong and Honolulu and later went to London to pursue the study of medicine. He was a man of wide vision, reading voluminously on many subjects. The subject that finally caught his full attention was the American and French Revolutions. He pondered hard and long over China's plight towards the end of the last century and came to the conclusion that only a revolution could overthrow the Manchu rule and put China on a democratic basis. With this in view, he gave up his medical practice and devoted all his time and faculty to the accomplishment of his objective. He first went to work among our overseas Chinese, knowing that they would be more ready to support his cause. With the ever growing number of Chinese students going to foreign countries, he directed his activities also to them wherever they were located. By word and printed pamphlets he solicited their support. He even risked his life by visiting China several times. There was already a price set on his head by the Manchu Government.

Although he successfully eluded several attempts to capture him in China, he was finally kidnapped in London and was kept at the Chinese Embassy awaiting arrangement to have him smuggled out of England and shipped to China. He was locked up in a small room on the third floor of the Embassy and had no means to send any message to his friends. He knew his old friend and teacher Dr. Cantlie was living near the Embassy. Scribbling a message on a piece of paper, he wrapped a five shilling coin with it, and addressing it to Dr. Cantlie, he tossed it through the window to the street. The message did reach the good doctor. He immediately went to the Foreign Office to inform the authorities of the unlawful kidnapping and holding of a political refugee. In characteristic efficiency the British Government demanded his immediate extradition and took appropriate steps to back up the demand. It was acceded to shortly after and he was set free to resume his life work for the emancipation of the Chinese people from an alien rule.

I had read a good deal about Dr. Sun before I met him for the first time in Tokyo. There and then I solemnly pledged to give my best for the furtherance of this cause. But for the breaking down of my health and the threat of being a victim to tuberculosis, I would still be in America when the Revolution broke out on the night of October 10, 1911. As it happened I was already in Shanghai. When the news came through that the Flag of Freedom was already unfurled in the triple cities of Hankow, Hanyang and Wuchang in the heart of China, our "workers" in Shanghai immediately went into action under the leadership of Mr. Chen Chi-mei. We attached and successfully took position of the headquarters of the Shanghai Garrison Commander. Simultaneously, the "workers" in other parts of China took similar actions. In less than a month the garrisons throughout China which took orders from the Manchu court in Peking crumpled like a box of matches. The revolutionary flag was hoisted in every provincial capital of the country. Dr. Sun was then still in America and did not return until towards the end of the year. General Li Yuan-hung, under whose leadership the revolutionary forces first raised the Flag of Freedom, was acclaimed as the leader of the whole revolutionary movement pending the return of Dr. Sun. A provisional central government was set up in Wuchang, the Capital of Hupeh province, with General Li at the head under the title of Generalissimo. I was sent to Wuchang to look after diplomatic affairs.

I think it would be necessary for me to digress from further recounting of the progress of the revolution and to present an analytic study of the reasons why the Manchu power which had entrenched itself for over two and half centuries, should fall so easily and rapidly.

On the whole the Manchu Emperors had not used despotic powers to govern the country. They followed and respected Chinese laws and customs, and had the knack to pick out Chinese with character and

Chapter 6   The 1911 Revolution

ability to be placed in the key positions of the government. But by the end of the last century an ambitious woman in the person of the notorious Empress Dowager Tze-hsi had usurped the powers of the Emperor. She was the second wife of Emperor Chia-ch'ing but dominated over the first wife who had the title of the Empress. By degrees she gained the title of Co-Empress and encouraged the Emperor to debauch himself so much so that he died quite young in age, so she was elevated to the rank of Empress Dowager when a young prince was installed as the Emperor. There was a nominal regent for the boy-Emperor but she exercised the supreme powers. Emperor Tung-chih also died quite young and another young prince was made Emperor. When Kwang-hsü first sat on the throne, he was a mere boy less than five years old, so the empress Dowager continued to dominate the court by "listening to political moves, behind the curtain."

After the Ts'ing dynasty was established in China, the Manchu Emperors had strict controls over the princes of the royal blood and saw to it that they were kept out of politics. This control began to be loosened during the machinations of the Empress Dowager. The fanatical Boxers would never have been permitted to run amok in Peking and nearby cities but for the Empress Dowager to listen to some of these young princes. Chinese statesmen of character and ability were sent out to distant provinces as Viceroys and Governors. Even the astute Yuan Shih-k'ai, who betrayed Emperor Kwang-hsü when the latter appealed to him for help in order to throw off the yoke around the Emperor's neck in the person of the Empress Dowager, was dismissed from the Court. All the important positions were then held by the young princes. This was a complete reversal of the old policy of keeping them out of politics, and constituted an important factor towards the liquidation of the Manchu dynasty.

A more potential factor was the rapid awakening of the Chinese people to the fact that they had an alien government over them. This was the result of the effective publicity work carried on by Dr. Sun Yat-sen and his co-workers in the Revolutionary Movement known as Chung Hsing Hui (中興會) which was organized among our overseas Chinese and thousands upon thousands of Chinese students who had migrated to Japan, America and other countries in the West. Upon the latters' return to their homeland they carried out their solemn oath to overthrow this alien overlordship. The name of the Movement due to political reasons was changed to Tung Meng Hui (同盟會) shortly before the actual unfurling of the Revolutionary Flag at Wuchang. The people of the whole country rose like one man and the Manchu garrisons and Chinese forces under their control surrendered en masse.

The death of the Empress Dowager, the "Old Fox" as she was nicknamed, at the turn of this present century, was another factor in the rapid disintegration of the Manchu power. Soon before her death, Emperor Kwang-hsü was also reported dead. There was strong suspicion that he was put out of the way at the order of the "Old Fox." Another young prince was installed as the Emperor Hsün-t'ung, the last Emperor of the Ts'ing dynasty, was destined to be a "Puppet Emperor" for life. After his abdication on the establishment of the Republic of China, he was allowed to remain in the old palace. With Japanese hobnobbing he was smuggled out of Peking and went to reside in the then Japanese concession in Tientsin. Later, when war broke out between China and Japan, he was proclaimed Emperor of the Japanese dominated Manchurian Empire, set up in the very ancestral home of the Manchus. After the surrender of the Japanese forces in Manchuria he was taken prisoner by the Russians and had remained in captivity ever since.

I will now continue with the progress of the Revolution. The nationwide response to the call for the overthrow of the Ts'ing dynasty so frightened the young princes that they had to recall Yuan Shih-k'ai back to power, not realizing that although undoubtedly he was a very able politician, he had no scruples about loyalty. Having gained a great reputation as the organizer of modern military forces stationed in North China and shown his political ability as the Governor of Shantung and later as Viceroy of the metropolitan provinces in North China, the young princes thought that they had a man who could stem the tide. He threw his best forces on the Hankow front, recapturing both Hankow and Hanyang and threatening also to retake Wuchang, then the seat of the Provisional Government of the Republic. In fact the situation was such as to lead Generalissimo Li Yuan-hung to believe that strategically it was best to evacuate Wuchang. Steps were already taken to move his forces further east, so as to join up with the revolutionary forces which were moving westward. Nanking was already in their hands, while Anking, the capital

Chapter 6   The 1911 Revolution

of Anhui province, and Nanchang, the capital of Kiangsi province, had also been captured by other revolutionary forces. Dr. Sun Yat-sen had now already returned to China. In a council of the leaders of the Revolution held in Nanking towards the end of 1911 a provisional constitution was proclaimed which provided among other organs of the Government, a provisional Senate, with representatives from every province of the country constituting it. The Senate was to elect a Provisional President and Vice-President. Nanking was declared the national capital of China. I was chosen as a representative from the province of Hupeh.

Just at this moment the wiry Yuan Shih-k'ai showed his skill in the game of politics. He threw out hints that internecine warfare could be avoided by setting up a "peace conference" between the revolutionary forces and his "Government" forces. His move had fooled most of the revolutionary leaders including Dr. Sun. The formula he suggested was that he would bring about the abdication of the Manchu Emperor in favor of a Republic but with himself to be elected as the President of the Republic. Dr. Sun had devoted his whole life to work for the overthrow of the Manchus and to set up a Republic and to bring peace and prosperity to his people and country. It was immaterial to him as to who should be at the head of the Republic, provided he be a Chinese national who should take a solemn oath to uphold the Republican form of Government and the Constitution. So it was arranged that such a conference be held at Shanghai. Meanwhile the organization of the Provisional Government went ahead. At the first meeting of the Senate Dr. Sun Yat-sen was elected Provisional President with General Li Yuan-hung Vice-President. Dr. Sun assumed his office on January 1st, 1912, by taking the solemn oath that he would defend the Republic and the upholding of the Constitution. This marked the beginning of the Republic of China.

Chapter 7

The Evolution of the Revolution

The so-called "Peace Conference" suggested by Yuan Shih-k'ai and accepted by Dr. Sun, took place in Shanghai at the beginning of 1912 after the arrival of Ms. Tong Shao-yi, a distinguished high official of the Ts'ing dynasty, who was one of the three groups of students sent to America in the early seventies of the last century and who had contributed a good deal in the reforms introduced and carried out by Yuan Shih-k'ai. He was a protégé and close friend of Yuan's, so his nomination as the Special Envoy to represent Yuan was fully accepted. Dr. Sun designated Dr. Wu Ting-fang, a recognized veteran diplomat, to represent the Republic. I was a student in America when Mr. Tong paid a state visit to Washington. Dr. Wu was then our Embassador there. I was among the students who were invited by our Embassador to meet Mr. Tong, so I came to know him personally. I was in Hankow when he arrived there, took him to call on Generalissimo Li Yuan-hung, and then accompanied him to Shanghai.

After a few meetings, the two envoys quickly came to terms and an agreement was duly signed. On February 12th an imperial edict was issued by the Manchu Court, and by the way it was the last imperial edict ever issued by a Manchu Emperor, stating the solemn abdication of the Emperor in favour of the Republic of China. It must have galled the inexperienced young Manchu princes to find themselves at the mercy of the man whom they had called back to power in the belief that he would be their savior. Dr. Sun, to carry out his part, sent in his resignation to the Provisional Senate and requested that Yuan Shih-k'ai be elected in his place. The Senate reluctantly but quickly acceded to his wish and Yuan Shih-k'ai was so elected with General Li Yuan-hung remaining as Vice-President of the Republic. There was a stipulation in the agreement that Yuan Shih-k'ai was to be

Chapter 7 The Evolution of the Revolution

installed as President of the Republic in Nanking and to take the solemn oath to defend the Republic and Constitution before the Senate at a special session.

There were great rejoicings throughout the nation, believing that the Revolution had obtained its objective. While it was true that the Revolution had ended the Manchu regime, even the political aspect of the Revolution was yet in the process of evolution. Usually, after a reigning dynasty was overturned, a new dynasty would take its place and the form of government would be patterned after the centuries-old monarchy. But this Revolution had brought about a democratic form of government, patterned after the American government, with an Executive Officer known as the President to be elected at stated intervals either by a popular vote of the people or by an electoral body with the electors chosen by the people, a Parliament on legislation, and a system of courts on judicial matters, generally known as the Executive Legislative and Judicial branches of the government. In addition, two new branches are to be organized, one to have control over the accounting and auditing of the finances of the central government as well as the provincial governments, and the other to supervise the behavior of the personnel of the government. Failing to find an appropriate English nomenclature to designate these branches of the government, the Chinese word or character "Yuan" (院) was adopted. The word connotes more than a Department or a Division of the Government. The English word Branch comes nearest to it but Yuan is more dignified than Branch. Hence the five Branches of the Government are called: Executive Yuan, Legislative Yuan, Judicial Yuan, Control Yuan, and Supervisory Yuan.

In the West, particularly in Great Britain and the United States of America, the tripartite form of government has been well established. Although the British have a King or Queen at the head of the government, the real executive powers are exercised by the Cabinet. The King still retains the power of veto over the actions of the Cabinet but for the last four centuries no British King had ever exercised that power. In America the President is the actual head of the government. His Cabinet ministers, generally known as Secretaries, are named and chosen by him with the consent and approval of the Senate. The British King is hereditary while the American President is elected every four years, and yet the British King only reigns but the

American President actually rules. With this major difference, the powers exercised by the Three Branches of the government are quite identical except on minor details. In both countries the power of control and supervision over the finances and personnel of the government have been exercised by Parliament or Congress respectively.

In China the exercise of all these powers had never been clear-cut. The Emperor was supposed to exercise all these powers. He not only reigned and ruled but his imperial edicts were considered as laws, judgments on judicial matters, promoting or cashiering of the officials, and what not. Yet, very few Emperors dared to be despotic in the exercise of his all-inclusive powers.

The western tripartite form of government is formulated on the principle of check and balance. The powers and functions of each branch of the government are clearly defined and scrupulously followed. They are in a way independent of each other and yet they are corelated. Each branch is to exercise its powers and functions without the interference of the other two. However, the Executive head, whether known as President, Premier or Prime Minister, in the selection and appointment of certain officials must have the consent and approval of the legislative body, the Senate as in the case of America or the House of Commons as in Great Britain. The legislative body formulates the laws but no enactment could become law without the signature of the Executive. In America it is known as the Executive veto. Still the legislative body could by a two-thirds majority pass over the Executive veto and declare the enactment as law. Similarly the judiciary body gives its judgments independent of the other two bodies, yet the judges in most cases are appointed by the Executive head with the consent and approval of the legislative body.

The Chinese government under the monarchs for over four thousand years had also followed the principle of check and balance, not so clearly defined as in a written constitution, but nevertheless had to follow an unwritten one like the British. The law of precedence had a powerful influence over the actions of governmental organs. Certain things had to be done in a certain way in order to conform to a precedent set down and practiced hitherto, deviation from which must have good reasons and the approval of the nation. In the West this approval is obtained by a popular vote of the people. In China hitherto it was gauged by the reaction of the people. If there were no opposition shown to a certain governmental action which deviated from former practices, the government would take it that the people had given their approval. But when opposition should be raised, the volume and size of the opposition formed the basis of partial or total rejection of such action. Once rejected, it set a new precedent for the guidance of succeeding governments.

The most powerful check on the behavior of the monarchs was the action of the Scholars of the land, generally known as the literati. Every monarch must appoint a number of the literati as Censors. They were paid by the government and their chief duty was to watch the actions of the government. If certain action of the government should deviate from or in direct opposition to a well recognized precedent, one or several of the Censors would present a strong memorial to the Emperor, outlining the reasons for censoring such an action. Should the Emperor turn a deaf ear to his or their joint memorial, then the literati throughout the land would hold meetings in their respective Literati Halls, whose deliberations could not be interfered by any government organ. Very few monarchs dared to oppose their actions. Even the most powerful Emperor Chin Shih Huang, that is the first Emperor and founder of the Chin dynasty, could not crush them. I have already related how this Emperor, in his attempt to silence them had buried three thousand of them alive after inviting them to a huge banquet. The massacre of such a large number of the leading scholars had absolutely no effect upon the whole body of the literati, who eventually succeeded in overthrowing the Chin dynasty under his successor. This set a strong precedent and I have no doubt that it constitutes the main refraining influence upon any monarch not to exercise his all-inclusive powers in a despotic way.

The leaders of the revolutionary movement believed that it would be better to have a written constitution for the country, wherein the powers and functions of the various branches of the government should be clearly stated. So the newly formed government of the Republic took steps at once to have an enactment by the Provisional Senate, setting forth how the Constitutional Assembly should be constituted and how its members should be elected. In my opinion a very grave mistake was committed in assigning dual responsibilities to this Assembly. It was to be composed of two Houses, the upper House known as the Senate and the lower House as the House. When sitting separately, they were to constitute the National Assembly, the Legislative Branch of the Government, while sitting as a whole they were to be the Constitutional Assembly to draw up and enact the written Constitution of the country.

There were to be elected ten Senators from each of the provinces together with an allotted number of Senators from those areas not considered as provinces, such as our overseas Chinese. The House was to have its members elected in numbers proportionate to the population of each province. In all there would be ____ [sic] in the Senate and ____ [sic] in the House. The elections were held towards the end of 1912. Great enthusiasm was shown by the people in their desire to retain their best "Sons" to represent them. It was the first time in the history of China that an election of this kind was ever held. Judging from the calibre of men who were chosen, either to the Senate or to the House, they were truly the elite of the people. Many of them had been educated abroad, some had held high government posts such as Viceroys and Governors and State Councillors, while others had won honours in the imperial examinations. But on account of the grave mistake in assigning to them the dual responsibilities, they failed miserably in that they were unable to enact a written Constitution for the country, which was primarily their first responsibility. Should they be assigned only to produce a written Constitution, I feel sure they would have succeeded.

In the first place they would not have any conflict with the Executive head, then held by Yuan Shih-k'ai after the resignation of Dr. Sun. President Yuan was of the old school and only had the experience of an executive, who wanted the powers of the President unlimited while the Constitutional Assembly maintained that there should be a proper balance of power between the Executive and Legislative branches of the government. Finding that the Assembly would not budge to give the President unlimited powers, he took steps to intimidate them, by arresting some of them on one pretext or another, until finally he outlawed the revolutionary party then known as Kuo Min Tang or the Nationalists. He was too shrewd to dissolve the Assembly. As the Nationalists had a large majority in it, the outlawing of them left only a small minority. Thus by browbeating and high-handed actions, the Assembly was rendered impossible to function. Although it was reconvened two years later after the unsuccess-

Chapter 7   The Evolution of the Revolution

ful attempt of Yuan Shih-k'ai to enthrone himself as the founder of a new dynasty followed by his death, nothing concrete was produced by it.

If the Assembly were given the sole task of the drafting of a written Constitution, it could have been held in Nanking or at any other place outside of the grip of Yuan Shih-k'ai. The draft when finally passed by the Assembly, would have been sent to the various provinces for ratification. After two-thirds of the provinces should have ratified it, it would have become the supreme law of the country, without any interference or obstruction from Yuan Shih-k'ai.

In the third place the number of members in the Assembly should not have been so large. Probably the size of the Senate would have been sufficient, giving each province ten representatives. The work of the Assembly would have thus been expedited. After the promulgation of the Constitution, a National Assembly should be called into existence. Their function would be primarily for the enactment of laws under the Constitution. This National Assembly should have two Houses as originally planned, with functions and powers of each House clearly stated, like the Senate and the House of the American Congress. There would have been greater progress in the evolution of the revolution for our country.

Chapter 8

Comical Tragedy

The comedy as staged in Peking by Yuan Shih-k'ai, after his election as the President of China but before his assumption of office, turned out to be a great tragedy both for himself and his country. In the agreement reached between Dr. Wu Ting-fang and Mr. Tong Shao-yi, it was understood that the newly elected President was to assume office in Nanking. Accordingly, a delegation was sent to Peking to welcome him to the National Seat of government and I was one of them. In our interview with the President-elect, he manifested every desire to have his inauguration in Nanking. He even enquired of us what kind of dress he should wear during the ceremony. We suggested that it would be appropriate for him to wear a morning coat with a top hat, as the American Presidents usually do during their inaugurations. The best tailor in Peking was sent for to get the outfit ready and every preparation seemed to be made for him to proceed to Nanking. The delegates were housed in the premises of the Peers' School and were well attended to as to our comfort and convenience.

Then on the night of February, a peal of thunder seemed to have come out from a clear blue sky. I was with two friends, one of them Dr. C. C. Wang also a delegate and the other my old friend Dr. W. C. Chen, at a restaurant near the Foreign Office. We had just seated in a cozy room and were giving orders to our waiter what we wanted for our supper. All of a sudden we heard shouts from the street, followed by volley after volley of rifleshots. All the lights at the restaurant were put out and the doors to the street were closed and barred. The city was lit up with huge fires raging in many parts of the city. On enquiry we were told that the crack Third Division had mutinied as a protest against requiring the President-elect to go to Nanking for his inauguration. To our great alarm we were further told that one of the barracks of this Division was right behind our restaurant! We were the only ones in the restaurant without queues and wearing western dress and would be easily spotted, if and when the military officers should come to arrest us. We had eaten nothing as our orders were not yet completely taken by the waiter. Besides, all the fires at the cooking-ranges had been put out for fear that any light would be seen from the street. In our excitement we did not feel any hunger at first, but as the night wore on and apparently we were not the objects of their attack, we began to feel both hungry and cold. Our stove had also been put out of fire, and it was in deep winter. In the midst of our misery and despair, in came a man of fairly large size to our room, and producing a pistol calmly informed us that he was sent to protect us. We did not say anything but in our minds we felt that our end was very near.

However, still nothing had happened to us. To our great relief we found our man soundly asleep on the K'ang, a native kiln in the form of a bed, which serves the double purpose of chairs or a bed, with the pistol on the table nearby. To satisfy our hunger we asked for and obtained several raw eggs and some bread and waited patiently for the break of day. At the first streak of dawn we woke up our man, gave him some money and told him to go and find out about the other members of our delegation, with an assurance that he would be further rewarded if he succeeded in getting the information we wanted. In a little over an hour he came back to inform us that all the delegates were unharmed and were gathered together at the Wagon Lits Hotel in the Legation quarters. Forthwith we proceeded to the hotel with him and found that he was not telling any yarn about it. We carried out our promise by giving him a substantial reward.

After a hearty breakfast I joined the deliberation of the delegation to see what course of action we should take next. Just then a high official was sent by the President-elect to express the latter's great concern over our safety and was much relieved that no harm had fallen to any of us. He pleaded with us to send a wire to Dr. Sun recommending that the inauguration be held in Peking instead, for fear of further mutinies of the soldiers in Peking and the surrounding districts. It was pointed out to us that the mutiny of the Third Division last night was broken up and put down with great difficulties. Should the other Division follow suit, it would be impossible for the President-elect to put it down with his meager body-guards. The plot was so well-laid and deftly carried out as to convince the whole delegation that such a request be wired to Dr. Sun. Being a reasonable man and a true patriot, the latter gave his consent accordingly. The inauguration ceremony took place in the western section of the Palace which was then being used to house the President-elect. The solemn oath of defending the Republic and the Constitution was duly taken and Dr. Sun was relieved of the duties and responsibilities of the President, not realizing at the moment that Yuan Shih-k'ai had a higher ambition than being the President of a Republic. He wanted to be the founder of a new dynasty. Yuan Shih-k'ai played his political games with a poker's face hard to match. He covered every move with the appearance of a true patriot, only wishing to do his best for the country, yet underneath it was toward his life dream of mounting the dragon throne.

After his inauguration as President of the Republic, he named Mr. Tong Shao-yi as the Premier with nine Cabinet Ministers, majority of whom were strong supporters of the Republic. However, he placed his own men in the key positions of the cabinet, namely, Ministers of Interior, Army and Finance Ministries, but these men enjoyed nationwide recognition as able and experienced administrative officials of the Ts'ing dynasty. So the Provisional Senate gave their consent and approval. I was appointed Vice-Minister of Commerce and Industry with Mr. Chen Chi-mei as the Minister. As Mr. Chen never assumed his office, I was made Acting Minister and had full responsibility for the organization and running of the ministry. Although Nanking was still the Capital of China, the Seat of the National Government was located in Peking, temporarily as it was understood in order to suit the situation. It was feared that there might have more mutinies of the army, if the Central Government should function in Nanking which would necessitate the President to reside there. He would then be surrounded with strong Republican military forces, even if he be granted to retain his own bodyguards. This was his second move in his political game to upset the Republic and to found a new dynasty.

His first move was to get back to power by having him recalled from retirement by the Manchu Court to help stem the tide of the Revolution. Once entrenched himself with the support of the Modern Divisions which he had brought about and quite well trained, he was in a position to bargain with the Republicans for the overthrow of the

Chapter 8   Comical Tragedy

Ts'ing dynasty. This was successfully accomplished through the "Peace Conference" held in Shanghai. The Manchu Emperor had to abdicate in favour of the Republic and he was duly elected President. Through that well-staged "mutiny of the Third Division" in Peking on the night of February, it was made "manifest" to Dr. Sun and the leaders of the Revolution, as well as to the whole nation, that it was imperative for him to remain in Peking, thus relieving him of his promise to go to Nanking for his inauguration. As a sequel to that move, it must necessarily follow that the Central Government should, for the time being at least, be located in Peking. He never contested the right of the Republican leaders to name Nanking as the new National Capital of the country. Had he done that his "hand" would have been shown and I am sure Dr. Sun would have called "the bluff." There might have more bloodshed in the ensuing conflict between the Republican forces and his Modern Divisions, but the outcome would have been decisive, and the tragedy, which finally brought ruin to him and did much damage to the progress of the country towards democracy, could have been avoided. Being a polished player of the political game, he abided his time and led the Republican leaders to believe that he was genuinely striving for the establishment of a democratic form of government in China.

Dr. Sun was much satisfied with the composition of the new Cabinet and with Mr. Tong Shao-yi at the head. He and Mr. Tong came from the same district and the latter was well-known for his progressive ideas. As a matter of fact most of the progressive measures undertaken by Yuan Shih-k'ai when he was our Resident High Commissioner in Korea, later as Governor of Shantung and Viceroy of the Metropolitan Northern Provinces, were initiated by Mr. Tong. Having been relieved from his duties as the President of the Republic and with his mind at ease, he spent a good part of the year in 1912 in visiting many sections of the country. Most of the provincial Governors were his staunch supporters in the Revolutionary movement. He wanted to renew their friendships and to get acquainted with their work and the general situation of the country. In some of these visits I had the pleasure as well as the honour of accompanying him.

Meanwhile steps were being taken to draft and enact laws for the election of our National Assembly, the first parliament ever to be instituted in China. This National Assembly consisted of two Houses, the Senate and the House. There were equal representatives in the Senate from each of the provinces with definite numbers of Senators assigned to those areas not recognized as provinces, while the representatives to the House were elected in proportion to the population of each province. Elections were held in accordance with the procedure set out by the laws.

On the surface there were no signs that President Yuan Shih-k'ai was concocting some new scheme to betray the Republic, but Premier Tong Shao-yi, when informed of it, strongly advised the President against it. It is true that he was a trusted friend of the President and would do everything to promote the latter's welfare but he knew much more about democratic form of government. After several unsuccessful attempts of Mr. Tong to persuade the President to refrain from taking such an action, he calmly informed the ministers at a Cabinet meeting that he intended to hand in his resignation. The majority of the cabinet ministers voted to hand in the resignation en bloc. No explanation was made by Mr. Tong for his resignation but he informed us that it was quite impossible for him to carry on the government any longer. To this day it had never been revealed what passed between the President and his chief minister which caused the latter's determination to quit his job. The significant thing was right after the handing in of the resignation of the cabinet, Mr. Tong left Peking immediately to take refuge in the British Concession in Tientsin. Years after Yuan Shih-k'ai's death, I happened to be visiting Mr. Tong in his home in Shanghai and casually asked him what was the cause of his resignation in 1912 and of his flight to Tientsin immediately following his resignation. He did not answer the first part of my question but remarked, "you did not know what that man was capable of," meaning of course that he would go to any limit in order to obtain his end. Subsequent events seem to show that Yuan Shih-k'ai must have confided to Mr. Tong of his scheme to establish a new dynasty, although Mr. Tong had been a lifelong and trusted friend of Yuan's and had served the Manchu Emperors for many years, he was at heart a true patriot. He could not betray the trust reposed in him by Dr. Sun in the upholding of the Republic and the Constitution. The assassination of two members of his cabinet, Mr. Sung Chiao-jen and Mr. Chen Chi-mei, in Shanghai, by Yuan's agents, explained the reason of his precipitate flight to Tientsin.

Chapter 8 Comical Tragedy

The resignation of the Cabinet must have little effect on the action of the President. Once more he abided his time. A veteran diplomat, Mr. Lu Tseng-hsiang, the Foreign Minister of the last Cabinet, was nominated the next Premier. Mr. Lu had been in foreign service for many years and had been recognized as a man of liberal views. So were most of the other members of the cabinet.

On April 18, 1913, the National Assembly held its inauguration meeting with the President of the Republic and the Cabinet members in full attendance. Previous to the inauguration meeting, the two Houses had chosen their respective President and Vice-President of the Senate and Speaker and Vice-Speaker of the House. Mr. Chang Chi was elected the President of the Senate and I the Vice-President. The Speaker of the House was Mr. Wu Ching-lien with Mr. _____ ? [*sic*] as Vice-Speaker. Mr. Chang was a native of Hopeh province, formerly Chihli, and I came from Chekiang while Mr. Wu hailed from Liaoning, formerly Fengtien, and Mr. _____ [*sic*] from Kweichow. So the north and south, east and west of the country were appropriately represented. The two Houses held a joint session for this occasion with the President of the Senate presiding. There were the usual speeches delivered by the President of the Republic, the Premier, and other dignitaries of the government. It is significant that on this day the Government of the United States of America extended its formal recognition to the Republic of China and her action was followed by the other Powers in due course. So the Republic of China became a full member of the family of Nations.

As the members of the National Assembly also constituted as members of the Constitutional Assembly and as they were charged with dual responsibilities, it was decided that certain days of the week should be set aside to devote their attention to the question of drafting and enactment of the Constitution for the country. A Drafting Committee with Mr. Tang Yi as chairman was duly appointed by the Constitutional Assembly and the Temple of Heaven was chosen as their place of meeting. The Temple of Heaven, being away from the centre of the city, is a place well fitted for their work, and the Committee went about it in all earnestness. In due course a Draft was ready and presented to the Constitutional Assembly for adoption. The first reading went through smoothly with a general debate on the Draft. Various amendments were put forward which were duly recorded for debate on the second reading when the Draft would be debated upon and passed clause by clause. Naturally it would require many sessions of the Assembly to complete its second reading. As a matter of fact the second reading of the Draft was never completed, due to the interference of the President of the Republic.

I have already pointed before that it was most unfortunate that the same men were to constitute both the National Assembly and the Constitutional Assembly. As a constitutional body they would not get into conflict with the Executive branch or any other branch of the Government. Their one and only concern was to produce a Constitution that would be approved by the people. But as a legislative body it was their duty to scrutinize the actions of the Government, particularly on its financial dealings. Yuan Shih-k'ai in his attempt to establish a new dynasty, as subsequent events proved it, was secretly arranging for big loans from all sources. The Japanese were the most willing to offer loans to him, for they had their own designs on China, among them the infamous Nishihara loans. Opposition to these loans began to manifest itself throughout the country and as spokesman of the people many members of the Assembly were outspoken in their opposition to contracting these loans. The President in order to suppress such opposition, took drastic measures by having over a dozen of them arrested on one pretext or another. Finding that these arrests could not intimidate them from further criticism and opposition, and particularly that the Constitution to be adopted contained clauses which would limit the powers of the Executive Branch on financial matters, he finally had to show his hand by outlawing the Kuo Min Tang or Nationalist party throughout the country. The first effect was felt by both the National Assembly and the Constitutional Assembly in that only a small minority was on hand in both Assemblies, leaving them impotent to function. But the effect on the nation was electric and opposition came from all parts of the country. Dr. Sun being the head of the outlawed Nationalist party had to take refuge in Japan. Once more he took the field to direct all the elements in the country for the upholding of the Constitution and down with Yuan Shih-k'ai.

Having shown his true colours, he could not now turn back but used all his resources to bring about a monarchical movement. He stuffed the two Assemblies with his own followers, produced a con-

Chapter 8   Comical Tragedy

stitution which gave the Executive supreme powers. He sent his trained forces southward and recaptured the provinces along the Yangtze river which had revolted against the government. So by the fall of 1914 the stage was set for him to mount the dragon throne which he had coveted ever since he was recalled to political power by the young Manchu princes after the Revolution broke out on October 10, 1911. Every political move he made since then was towards that end, but he played his game so adroitly that no one could suspect or detect his real intentions at first. The "Peace Conference" held in Shanghai was the means to oust the Manchu Emperor and to get his own election as the President of the Republic. The staged mutiny in Peking was to convince the Revolutionary leaders to believe that it was unwise to ask him to proceed to Nanking for his inauguration and that Peking was to continue for the time being at least as the Seat of the National Government. The appointment of a liberal cabinet with Mr. Tong Shao-yi as the Premier was to show to the nation what a genuine supporter he was for a democratic form of government. The break came when Mr. Tong and his cabinet handed in their resignation en bloc, yet he was shrewd enough to allow the election of the National Assembly to take place and to hold sessions in Peking to have a written Constitution drafted and promulgated. Only when he discovered that this Assembly would not write a constitution to suit his purpose that he was forced to show his true colours. By then the Republic of China was already recognized by most, if not all of the countries of the world and he had succeeded in getting big loans to back up his next move to be enthroned as the "Emperor" of China.

In all his maneuver, he miscalculated that the time had changed. The forces of democracy were gaining strength all over the world. He would not be able to turn the clock backwards. Had he lived couple of centuries earlier, he might have succeeded to found a new dynasty. While his military forces were being used in middle China to recapture the provinces which first resisted his outlawing of the Nationalist party, the outlying province of Yunnan in the southwest corner of the country raised the clarion voice calling upon the whole nation to resist his imperial designs. It spread like wildfire. Soon the whole nation was up in arms and the Modern Divisions he had so laboriously trained and brought into being were no match to the nationwide opposition. Everything was made ready for his crowning as the new

"Emperor" of China but it never came off. He died of a broken heart. So ended this comic tragedy. With his superb ability as an administrator, what a great President he would have made and what great progress he could have accomplished for his country and his people!

Chapter 9

Interregnum

After the death of Yuan Shih-k'ai, Gen. Li Yuan-hung as Vice-President of the Republic assumed the office of the Chief Executive, but he was in a very difficult situation. The opposition to the Yuan regime did not soften even after his death, inasmuch as his strong coterie of supporters were still holding important government positions, particularly, the military elements who backed him in his aspirations to mount the throne. It is true that President Li did cancel the order outlawing the Nationalist party and recall both the National and Constitutional Assemblies to resume their unfinished tasks. In due course both Assemblies were reconvened to take up their work from where it was abruptly interrupted by Yuan's autocractic[autocratic] action, but it was plain that very little could be accomplished. The country was already in the process of disintegration. Powerful warlords seized the initiative to govern the provinces in their own way, paying in certain cases only lip-service to the National government while in others it was outright independence. Particularly it was so with Gen. Chang Tso-lin (張作霖) who had entrenched himself in the three northeastern provinces of Liaoning (formerly Fengtien), Kirin and Heilungkiang, formerly known as Manchuria, the home of the Manchus. Strong satraps were set up in various parts of the country, especially in the outlying provinces. It is to be noted that a province in China is often larger than a country in Europe. The province of Szechuan, for instance, is larger than Germany both in size and population.

With practically an empty national coffer and with the country so badly torn up and divided, President Li could not make much headway in his efforts to pacify the nation. I was back in Peking when the Assemblies were reconvened. During the sessions before the Assemblies were broken up by Yuan Shih-k'ai, I had to preside over the Senate due to the absence of its President, Mr. Chang Chi, as well as over the Constitutional Assembly. At the reconvening of the Assemblies Mr. Chang Chi tendered his resignation, and a new President of the Senate was elected in the person of Mr. Wang Chia-hsiang (王家襄), so my work was not so arduous as before. I gave a good deal of my time then to the promotion of athletic activities and social work, such as the Young Men's Christian Association and the Red Cross Society. In fact I derived greater pleasure in rendering these social services than either in the Government or in the Assembly.

In the midst of President Li's efforts to unify the country, a new element was added to the political strives. Gen. Chang Hsün was then in command of quite a strong military force stationed in Hopeh, one of the Metropolitan Provinces formerly under the Viceroy of Peiyang. He got into his head a notion that the only way to unify the country was to reinstate the Manchu Emperor Hsüan T'ung on the Throne. Without giving any warning, he marched at the head of his force towards Peking and having overpowered the garrisons on the way, he gained possession of the Capital on _____? [*sic*] His movement was so sudden as to give very little time for other forces to come to Peking for its defence, but fortunately there was enough time for the Government to evacuate the Capital. The members of the two Assemblies, being the main target of this Monarchical attack, had to scramble out of Peking in all haste. I had to disguise myself as a farmer and took a cart to take me to Tungchow on the Grand Canal, there to take a boat ride to Tientsin, knowing that the railway between Peking and Tientsin must have been occupied by Chang Hsün's forces. I left Peking just as the gates of the city were opened early that morning and in the nick of time. Chang Hsün reached the Capital the very same day.

Gen. Tuan Chi-jui had been the Minister of War in Mr. Tong's cabinet and was a close friend of Yuan Shih-k'ai's. Like Mr. Tong he was a strong supporter of the Republic, and although he did not break away from Yuan as Mr. Tong did and remained as the War minister in the subsequent cabinet, he was not in favour of a monarchical form of government. He was quite a discreet man and seemed only to mind his own business to look after military matters, leaving political questions to the President to decide. He maintained this attitude right through Yuan's regime and even after his death. But as soon as he learned of Chang Hsün's coup d'état, he quietly left Peking and marshaled his forces in the adjacent cities and then conveyed on the Capital. Chang Hsün's men were no match to his well trained forces and the ill-advised General had in turn to flee himself, so this short-lived monarchical movement was ended as sudden as it was started.

In spite of this rapid collapse of a movement for the re-installation of monarchy, there was not much headway in the effort of the Central Government to pacify and unify the country. Most of the provinces or combinations of provinces were under the rule of the Warlords. They did not flatly disobey the orders of the National authorities. Certain national organs were able to function as heretofore, such as the Maritime Customs, the postal service, the judicial courts and to a certain extent the Salt Gabelle. But each Warlord was practically independent of the Central Government. At times they even carried on military feuds with their neighbouring provinces. The most notable instances were the "Wars" between Gen. Wu Pei-fu of the Chihli (or Hopeh) faction against Gen. Chang Tso-lin of the Fengtien (or Liaoning) clique, and between Gen. Lu Yung-hsiang of Chekiang and General Chi Hsieh-yuan of Kiangsu. In each case the defeated General simply relinquished his command and a new Warlord took his place and the situation remained as before.

Europe was then in the grip of the so-called First World War. German invasion of France through a break in Belgium was at its height and Great Britain, both to carry out the terms of the "Entente Cordiale" and to come to her own defence, had declared war on Germany. The units of these two naval Powers came to grips in several naval engagements not only in the British Channel and the North Sea but in practically every ocean on the globe. By having Turkey as her ally German forces were also threatening the Suez Canal and the Near East. The United States of America was still then maintaining her neutrality, but her sympathy was entirely with Great Britain. Japan lined up with the Allies after Great Britain declared war on Germany and in a lightening-like move struck at the German base in the Shantung peninsula, where Germany had acquired extensive mining and railway rights from China besides the port city of Tsingtao after the Boxer Outbreak. The British had sent a token force to aid the Japanese. After a short campaign the Germans were entirely eliminated from the foothold in Asia. Japan then took over all the rights which the Germans had extorted from China.

Such was the state of affairs in China in particular and in the world in general. Although China was much divided internally, she was still recognized as a member of the family of nations. Dr. Sun was, however, very much disturbed over the internal situation in China. In ousting the Manchu regime, his one object was to build up a strong and united China. Yuan's betrayal of the Republic followed by the setting up of Warlords in the various parts of the country after his death, tended to weaken the country instead of building her up. The only way to unify the nation was to have a strong central government reestablished, having authority over the provinces in foreign affairs, national finances, judicial courts, communications such as railways, postal and telegrams, and the army and navy, allowing the provinces to exercise authority over provincial and local affairs. With this program in view he launched his campaign by ousting the Warlord in Kwangtung, Gen. Lung Chi-kwang. The Chinese navy under Admiral Cheng Pi-kwang was the first to come forward to carry out his program. After the capture of Canton, the Capital of the province, a provisional Central Government was set up and veteran statesmen like Mr. Tong Shao-yi and Dr. Wu Ting-fang were invited to join the new movement. Important members of the defunct National Assembly were also called to Canton to assist Dr. Sun with Mr. Wu Ching-lien, the Speaker of the House and myself, Vice-President of the Senate leading them. A college for the training of officers to staff the new army to be created was established at Whampoa, at the estuary of the Pearl River, not far from Canton. General Chiang Kai-shek was appointed President of this College.

Much was being accomplished during the two following years. We did not want to disrupt China's diplomatic relations with the other countries, so we let Peking handle all such matters. When America was finally drawn into the conflict with Germany, we made strong representations to Peking to back up China's declaration of war on Germany by sending a substantial force to Europe to assist the Allies in their life and death struggle against a formidable enemy. However, Peking turned a deaf ear to our representations. But we felt very strongly that unless we had our units fighting in the front lines of the war, we would have no voice at a subsequent peace conference, or a feeble voice at the best.

Chapter 9 Interregnum

Under the energetic leadership of General Chiang Kai-shek several Divisions of the new Army were whipped into shape. It was proposed that we should send three of these Divisions to Europe, since Peking refused to undertake the task. I was commissioned to proceed to Washington to negotiate with the American government on this project. I had Mr. Quo Tai-chi and Mr. Eugene Chen to assist me in this most delicate diplomatic mission. On the one hand we did not want to give the impression to the American government in particular and to the other Allied governments in general that we handled diplomatic matters independent of Peking, and yet on the other hand it was manifest that the offer of sending Chinese military forces came from the "Southern" government and not from the "Northern," as Canton and Peking were so dubbed in the eyes of the world. So our first step was to get a tacit consent from Peking before we undertook the mission. This would enable our diplomatic official in Washington to accord to us any assistance that we might stand in need.

Armed with this assurance from Peking our mission sailed on one of the Dollar Line boats, now known as the President Line, in May, 1918. In those days traveling was slow. It took us nearly a month to reach Washington. Dr. Alfred Shao-ki Sze was our Minister to the American government. We put all the cards before him as we found him most sympathetic to the purpose of our mission. Although appointed by the so-called "Northern" government, he felt very keenly that he was representing the whole of China. He saw eye-to-eye with us in the importance of having our men fighting in the ranks of the Allied forces which were hammering tellingly on the German military machine. He paved the way for us to interview the then Secretary of State, Mr. Philander Knox. We had many sessions with him and finally he agreed on behalf of his government to arrange for transport to ship our men to Europe. While the American government was making ready to have ships go to China, General Chiang had made the final touches to get the three Divisions ready for overseas services. Nobody knew that the German military machine would crack so soon. The Germans have always been good soldiers, able to sustain lots of punishments, but apparently they had enough of them and so on November 11, that year the German Command gave up the struggle and sued for peace. When this news was flashed all over the world, the Allied countries were jubilant over their victory. We were still in Washington when this news reached America. The street scenes there were beyond description. People literally danced for joy. Men and women, though unknown to each other, would hug and kiss, shout and dance, behaving like children in their ecstasy. We were naturally in deep sympathy with their state of mind. Parents were thinking of their boys soon to return home, wives of their husbands, and young girls of their sweethearts. But we felt what a golden opportunity China had lost in coming to the front as a world power by being too late to have a share in overpowering the haughty German Emperor, Wilhelm II, and his powerful military machine. I personally seldom shed tears but on this occasion I could not help weeping copiously, though silently.

Chapter 10

The Paris Peace Conference

After the end of the First World War, all the eyes of the world capitals turned to Paris where the Peace Conference was to be held. China, being one of the Allied nations, was naturally also invited to participate at its deliberations. As anticipated by those of us who felt strongly that China should have sent fighting units in order to have a stronger voice in shaping the peace treaties with Germany and her Associated States, we were given the place of a third-rate Power. The five leading Powers, namely, Great Britain, the United States of America, France, Italy and Japan, were each awarded five seats, while Belgium, Brazil and Serbia were represented by three delegates each. China was only to have two seats, in spite of the size of our country and our unlimited manpower. We had large labour battalions on the fields of battle and their efficiency and bravery were acknowledged by the commanding generals, but unfortunately for China these men were not sent by our government but recruited by other Allied countries, particularly Great Britain. However, those of them who fell on the battle fields, had made their contributions in defeating the enemies, and they had not died in vain.

In order to keep a united front in dealing with the other nations of the World, both Peking and Canton agreed to send a joint delegation to the Peace Conference. With Mr. Lu-Tseng-hsiang, our veteran diplomat, heading it, I was appointed its second delegate. In addition to Mr. Quo Tai-chi and Mr. Eugene Chen, Canton also appointed Mr. Wu Chao-chu, son of Dr. Wu Ting-fang, to be on the delegation. Mr. Quo and Mr. Chen were already in the United States with me when the war ended, so we awaited the arrival of Mr. Lu before we sailed for France. Dr. V. K. Wellington Koo, our Minister to Great Britain, Dr. Alfred Shao-ki Sze, our Minister to the United States of America, and Mr. Wei Shun-tsu, our Minister to Belgium, were also appointed by Peking as members of our delegation. Mr. Lu reached America just before the end of the year, so our delegation sailed on S. S. George Washington on January 1, 1919. Mr. Franklin D. Roosevelt, then Assistant Secretary of Navy and Mrs. Roosevelt were also on board and they played the part of hosts to us on our way across the Atlantic not realizing then that they were destined to be the President of that great Republic and its First Lady. When I was sent to America as China's Ambassador in 1937, Mr. Roosevelt was then the President and we exchanged vivid and pleasant recollections of our voyage together on S. S. George Washington.

Mr. Hoo Wei-teh was then our Minister to France. He had quite a long career in diplomacy, having been our Minister to Japan and Russia. So his son, Mr. Victor Hoo is one of our best linguists, able to speak French, English and German quite fluently and with talking knowledge of both Japanese and Russian. The elder Mr. Hoo was very much a scholar himself and besides he was always a good host. Having missed Chinese food for quite a while, we went very often to our legation to regale ourselves with tasty Chinese dishes. Our delegation with a little over thirty people made Hotel Lutetia our headquarters which was not far from our legation.

Each delegation from the Allied countries had its problems to solve. I am not going to discuss the problems of other countries. They were many and varied, except when they entangled with ours. Our main problem was over Japan's occupation of Tsingtao and her taking over of the mining and railway rights which Germany had exacted from China as concessions. Japan had no right whatever to claim them as "spoils of war," for not only there was no war between China and Japan but both countries were allies of the same war against Germany. We had several other problems which had to be straightened out with other countries, chief among them being customs autonomy, extraterritorial rights, foreign courts and other concessions. The whole thing could be summarized in the question of the revision of the unequal treaties that had been entered into by China under the defunct Manchu regime. These unequal treaties had robbed China of many of her sovereign rights. We were conscious that these problems did not come within the competency of the Peace Conference, but at such an international gathering we considered that it was the right place to bring these problems before the nations of the world. Accordingly a dossier was prepared, entitled the Case of China, and presented to the Conference. We knew there would be no action taken by it but the way would be prepared for China to take diplomatic actions looking for the revision of the unequal treaties. So we concentrated our attention on our main problem, namely to get Japan out of the Shantung peninsula.

The delegates of the leading Powers were naturally engrossed with questions vis-à-vis Germany. It took over five months for these questions to be discussed and debated upon before it was possible to have a draft of the Peace Treaty ready to be handed to the German delegation. The Germans, being the defeated in the war, had no voice in the shaping of the treaty. When the final draft was ready they were called in to attend the Conference. They were either to accept or reject it. Rejection would mean the re-opening of war and Germany was in no position to continue the combat, so they had to accept it in toto, just like signing a blank check. As a matter of fact the reparations exacted by the Allies from Germany were not exactly in figures but a general statement as much as the Allies had suffered in losses in the conflict.

Another element came in to prolong the time in the making of the treaty. There was to be attached as part of the treaty a Covenant of the League of Nations. President Woodrow Wilson was attending the Conference as the head of the American delegation. It was largely his pet idea that the League Covenant should be made a part of the peace treaty. It was generally admitted that the world was in great need of a world organization to prevent any further world wars. The war just over had cost so much in life and property. The victors suffered just as much as the defeated nations, excepting the honour of being victorious. That there was much weakness in the Covenant to bring about the desired effect was generally admitted. However, it was an attempt well worth trying out. The great blunder was to make it a part of the peace treaty, as it proved to be in the case of the United States when the treaty was presented to the Senate for ratification and was rejected. So America was out of the League of Nations before the League came into function. So many factors had come into the picture which require a detailed analysis before it could be made clear.

Very few people would link the rejection of the peace treaty by the American Senate with the Fiume question. Fiume, better known as Trieste, is the port at the head of the Adriatic Sea. It was a bone of contention between Italy and Yugoslavia. For centuries the Slavs had been living in this area, but as the Italians expanded their world trade, many Italian merchants moved into Fiume so as to tap the trade of the hinterland through the Adriatic Sea and the Mediterranean Sea into the world routes on the high seas of the globe. The Italian government after the conclusion of the war claimed that the port should be awarded to Italy as a reward for her part in defeating Germany and her Associates of which Yugoslavia was one. The other Allied nations believed that it should be retained by Yugoslavia. When it was finally decided to write into the treaty to let Yugoslavia retain the port, the whole Italian delegation, led by Mr. Orlando, walked out of the Conference. So out of the five great Powers at the Conference only four were left.

The contention over the Shantung peninsula between China and Japan was giving also a great headache to the Big Five. America had insisted right through the debates that it should be returned to its rightful owner, China. The walkout of the Italian delegation gave the Japanese a golden opportunity to stage a similar walkout, but they were shrewd enough not to make this issue as the reason for quitting the Conference. Subtly, they brought forward the question of the American discrimination against the Yellow race at the Conference and had a motion tabled for debate. Unless this race discrimination should be righted, they threatened that they would also walk out of the Conference. President Wilson was quite disturbed over this move, knowing it would be impossible for him to bring about a revision of the existing laws. To have another of the five powers walk out on it might wreck the whole Conference. In secret talks with the head of the Japanese delegation, he found that they would withdraw their motion for a debate on the American discrimination against the Yellow race, if the Shantung peninsula should be decided in her favour, which would be naturally opposed by China.

In his anxiety to save the Conference whereby the Covenant of the League of Nations could be accepted by all the participating nations, he turned to our delegation looking for concession from us. He sent his legal advisor, Mr. Williams, to plead with us to agree to the clauses in the treaty concerning the transfer of German rights in Shantung to the Japanese with the assurance that the President would take diplomatic action after the signing of the treaty to induce the

Chapter 10 The Paris Peace Conference

Japanese to return these rights to China. We pointed out to Mr. Williams that by signing the treaty with these clauses would bind China to honour them, while Japan would not be bound to return them to China. We suggested that another clause be added to the effect that Japan would in turn restitute these rights to China within a definite specified period. Failing that, we would ask President Wilson to send to us a note through the State Department to our Foreign Office giving this assurance as verbally conveyed to us through Mr. Williams. When he gave us the answer the next day that neither alternative could be complied with, we told him that the only course left for us was to refrain from signing the treaty altogether.

Externally great pressure was brought to bear on us by the French and British delegations particularly the French urging us to agree to sign the treaty as drafted with the objectionable clauses which we opposed most vehemently. The French Premier, Mr. Clemenceau, who was also head of the French delegation repeatedly sent his Chief Secretary to negotiate with us on this burning question. As we were as anxious as the other delegations to have the treaty completed and duly signed, we made several suggestions on the modus vivendi so that a way could be found to have the treaty to be signed by China without binding her to recognize the clauses concerned. One suggestion was to have a statement inserted by us when signing the treaty to the effect that we did not agree to these clauses. Another suggestion was that a written statement to that effect was to be handed to each delegation before the treaty was signed. When both of these suggestions were rejected by Mr. Clemenceau, we made it clear to him that we had no other course open but to refuse to sign the treaty.

Internally, since our delegation was made up of representatives from both the "northern" and the "southern" governments, it was most essential that we put up a united front on this crucial matter. We learned that Peking was rather "indifferent" to the question and gave instructions to the delegates to use their own judgment. The "southern" delegates had clear cut instructions never to sign another treaty giving away any concessions detrimental to the interests of our country. So a meeting of all the delegates was arranged and a secret ballot be taken. When the votes were counted every one voted for the rejection of the treaty with the objectionable clauses, with one blank vote, the voter seemed to be unable to take a decided stand. I believe at heart he was also for the rejection but was not courageous enough to put in his vote accordingly.

This unanimous decision was of tremendous importance to the future conduct in the foreign affairs of China. Whatever differences our people might have concerning domestic problems, we were united on the question of recovering our full sovereign rights. This courageous decision paved the way for later negotiations with practically all the nations of the world for the revision of the unequal treaties entered into by China under the Manchu regime. I did not realize then that this important task should fall on my shoulders, and I was glad with the blessings of God and the support of my fellow countrymen, I was able to bring it to a successful conclusion during the four terms when I was at the head of the Foreign Office.

On June 28, 1919, the Palace at Versailles was gaily decorated for the signing of the Peace Treaty by the Allied Delegates with the German representatives. Each delegate had a seat assigned to him. There were two seats for the Chinese delegates, but they were empty! Mr. Lu and I did not turn up at all. It was a great surprise to the other delegates, particularly to the "Tiger," (Mr. Clemenceau's nickname) who was presiding over the meeting. He was under the impression that we would weaken at the last minute and meekly turn up to sign our names on the dotted lines.

We expected some disciplinary action by the Conference for our refusal to sign the treaty. Favorable reaction from the world press and the united support of our whole nation apparently had prevented the Conference leaders from taking any positive action. We continued to take part in the Conference deliberations over the Austro-Hungarian, Turkish and the other associates of the Germans. As there was little, if any, controversy, in so far as China was concerned, we duly signed those treaties as drafted by the Conference. Because of our refusal to sign the peace treaty with the Germans, China was still, technically speaking, at war with Germany. China and Germany eventually concluded a peace treaty, embodying what was in the original treaty signed at Versailles minus the objected clauses concerning German rights in Shantung. This highly controversial subject had been already disposed of in a subsequent agreement made between China and Japan, through the good offices of the United States, in which Japan agreed to return to China all the German rights in Shantung.

Chapter 10   The Paris Peace Conference

I had to take a very active part in guiding our own delegation to take the right steps in our deliberations with the different delegations concerned over the controversial questions involved. Our Chief delegate Mr. Lu was in very poor health and was hospitalized several times during the summer months of 1919. So in the fall I asked for a month of leave and spent most of it in England. Although I had visited this beautiful Isle several times before, the first being in 1909 when I was still studying at Yale but was sent to England to attend a students' conference at Oxford, I never had the opportunity to see the country at large. I stayed with some Chinese friends who had lived in England for some time. So they guided me to see many parts of the British Isles. I was then a gentleman at leisure, free from any responsibility, but my vacation was cut short while visiting the historical sights in Edinburgh. A wire came from our delegation urging me to return to Paris to head our delegation in the first celebration of the Allies on the Armstice [Armistice] Day, November 11. Mr. Lu was then still in a hospital. Reluctantly I gave up my vacation and plunged once more into the activities of our delegation, till we sailed from Marseilles towards the end of the year when the Peace Conference was all over.

Chapter 11

Social Services

That China stands in great need of social services is very evident. The plight of the bulk of her population is such which calls for help in many directions. Physically, they are suffering from the ravages of many diseases, particularly tuberculosis and trachoma. The death rate of tuberculosis is awfully high, while trachoma made many blind, though very few people died of it. At the same time it is also quite evident that there is much latent good will in the hearts of our people. This good will unfortunately manifests itself mostly after calamity has befallen on the victims in the form of providing free coffins to those who died in poverty or free hospitals or medicine to the sick.

Mentally, many of our people are denied an opportunity to get an education even of the elementary grade. The percentage of the illiterate is appallingly high. It is in a way fortunate for China that over 85% of our people are engaged in farming and tilling of the land. Lack of education is not so much felt there. Still, if our farmers were literate enough to get the benefit of science through published books and magazines, what greater improvements could be made in the care of the crops, thereby increasing their volumes and giving them larger returns. While it is true that the government must provide for the elementary education of the children of school age, yet the demand for such education must come from the people themselves. This calls for the social service workers to convince the parents of these children the need and value of such education and to create that demand.

Spiritually, our people lack positive actions in religious education. Of the five principal religions of the world, China is the home of two of them, Taoism and Confucianism. There is no question that these two religious teachings have made their impresses upon our people, have made them what they are. Lao-Tze, the founder of Taoism, had taught our people to know the Truth and the Way of Life, leading to

Chapter 11   Social Services

the Truth. He used the word Tao which literally means the Way, the Road. The best equivalent of the word is the Greek word Logos. Lao-Tze's interpretation of Tao exactly coincides with St. John's declaration: "In the beginning was Logos, and Logos was with God, and Logos was God." His teachings are highly mystic. To understand them one must do a good deal of meditation and searching of one's heart. Confucius, on the other hand, laid emphasis on the right living, to be in harmony with God. He used the word T'ien to designate God. Literally, T'ien means Heaven and conforms with the Christian conception of Heaven, the Home of the Blessed, where God resides and where He receives all His faithful and righteous children.

In the teachings of both Lao-Tze and Confucius there was no positive action in bringing their messages to the people at large. They were couched in beautiful classical language but only the educated could study them. Anyone whose education enables him to have a close study of these cannot but be deeply impressed with their lofty ideas and ideals, inevitably leading men to know God, His love for mankind and His desire that His children should love one another, be good and pure and do good. Unfortunately their teachings could only reach the few who have the privilege to have an access to them. What a great difference there is between the way their teachings are brought to the attention of mankind and that of Christianity! Jesus Christ gave this final message to His disciples: "Go ye therefore, and teach all nations, baptizing them in the name of the Father, and of the Son, and of the Holy Ghost." Here you have positive action to bring the knowledge of God to all mankind, whether educated or not. The teachings of Mohammed are spread abroad in the same positive way. Once a week those of the same faith would meet in their churches or mosques, worshipping God or Allah, as the case maybe, and listening to learned scholars propounding the deep truth in simple language. Moreover, mission societies were formed whose emissaries, generally known as missionaries, went to the end of the earth to preach God's message of love and joy to the world. We have yet to find any Taoist or Confucianist Missions sent abroad to bring their teachings to the peoples of the other countries. Even at home in China while the Taoists have temples of some kind where it is more for meditation than for preaching and propaganda, the Confucianists have only temples to commemorate the Great Sage. The Buddhists are not so positive as the Christians and the Mohammedans but they have temples which are open to the public every day of the year attracting huge crowds to worship in them and they did send Buddhists missions to the other lands, notably to China and Japan.

As I was born in a Christian family and embraced the Christian faith early in life, I have been always in favour of positive action to work for better conditions for my people. I believe strongly that there is much latent good will in the hearts of my people. What is needed is to marshal forces to bring out that good will and put it into social service, and the starting point is to work for and with the young men and women throughout the country. Hence my strong support for the work of the Young Men's Christian Association movement when it was started in China towards the end of last century. The triangle is a fitting sign for the Association. It is to work for the uplifting of the physical, mental and spiritual sides of a man. Each side has to be built up and strengthened every day of his life. That is why in the Y. M. C. A. centre, provisions are made for physical development in the way of gymnasiums, swimming pools and athletic fields; for mental work, schools, day and night classes; and for spiritual welfare, prayer meetings, bible classes, lectures and discussion groups.

The growth of the Y. M. C. A. Movement in China has been phenomenal. The same may be said of its sister organization the Y. W. C. A.. In a short time it has spread all over the country, attracting thousands upon thousands of young men to take active parts in its work. From the start three principles have been laid down to ensure permanency of its work. First, before organizing a Y. M. C. A. in a given locality, a survey must be made whether there is sufficient Christian leadership for the starting of a Y. M. C. A.. It is considered essential that religious faith and enthusiasm must furnish the vital motive power to its growth. Secondly, is the community sufficiently strong in financing this enterprise? Each local Association must draw its financial support from its own members in the form of membership fees and donations. It is not permitted to seek financial support from other communities for its annual budgets. The third requirement, and it is considered most vital, is that there must be sufficient trained personnel to handle the affairs of the Association, known as the Secretaries, and they are paid officers of the Association for their services. Hence much attention is given to their enlistment and training before they

Chapter 11 Social Services

are assigned to their fields of activities. Failing in any one of these three requirements would prevent the National Committee from granting a charter for the organization of a new Association. It is to be noted that only in a few cases when an Association, once organized and granted a charter, failed eventually to function properly, and it was due largely to the faulty judgment of the man or men making the survey.

The work of the Y. M. C. A. affords a wonderful opportunity to our young men to render social services to the communities. The annual membership campaign is a great training centre for leadership and team work for these young men. It generates enthusiasm to attract other young men to join in the activities of the Association and to tap their resources for the support of a worthy cause. From the experiences gained in the activities of the Association, many of them become prominent in other fields of social services, such as athletics, medical work, social and moral welfare movements, and a number become pastors after embracing the Christian faith and receiving a required course in theology.

I consider the work of the Y. M. C. A. type most constructive. It tends to develop all the three essential parts of a man, his body, his mind and his spirit. But other organizations which aim to specialize any one of them are also worthy of our support. From my own personal experience I have come to know the value of athletic activities to the building up of one's body and keep it strong and healthy. So in conjunction with Dr. Chang Po-ling and other friends we began to promote athletic competitions. I met Dr. Chang when we were both students on the field of a football match. I was then studying at the Peiyang University while he was a student of the Naval College in Tientsin. A football match was arranged for our two teams representing each educational institution. Ever since we collaborated in the promotion of athletics. Eventually, the China National Amateur Athletic Federation was organized with branches all over the country. Besides promoting local competitions, a National Meet was held every two years, rotating in such cities which could furnish the facilities for such a meet. The First National meet was held in ____ [sic] in ____ [sic]. Subsequently, we joined the International Olympic Games under the auspices of the International Olympic Committee. We sent one athlete to the Los Angeles Meet in 1932. Later in 1936 and 1948 we sent quite a substantial team to Berlin and London respectively. In ____ [*sic*] our C. N. A. A. F. made an arrangement with the Athletic organizations in Japan and the Philippines to have a periodical contest between the athletes of the three countries, known as the Asian Games. This arrangement would have included India, Indonesia and other Asia countries but for the breaking out of the Second World War. The Asia Games now do include them and other Asia countries. Looking back over the half century since we first promoted athletic activities, we find a steady improvement in the physical welfare of our people and it is my profound hope that future generations will have better physique and greater enjoyment in life through athletics.

Another phase of social service for our people is to help organizations which give direct relief to those of our fellow citizens when calamites fall upon them, such as flood, fire, epidemics, or even as a result of war. There are outstanding organizations doing such direct relief work, among them I may mention a few most prominently known to us. The Red Cross Society, though originated as a result of the Crimean War through the efforts of Miss Florence Nightingale, is now a world organization to do relief work in time of peace as well as of war. The first Red Cross Society in China was organized by Mr. Shen Tien-ho in Shanghai in ____ [*sic*]. Its object appeals to our people as worthy of support as it does to other nations. Soon similar organizations sprang up in the larger cities of the country and China was admitted into the membership of International Red Cross. Dr. W. W. Yen, one of our most prominent diplomats, was President of the China Red Cross for many years. I had the honour of being its President for several terms also.

Another well-known relief organization in China of a national scope is the Red Swastika Society. It came into existence only a little more than forty years ago but it gained a momentum even greater than the Red Cross in so far as China is concerned. This Society is both a religious as well as a philanthropic organization. Its work aims at two definite objects, one to emphasize the spiritual rejuvenation of its members and the other to intensify their deeds of benevolence. It is religious in that its members are constantly reminded of the Presence of God in their daily life. It does not preach any new doctrine or religious belief, for it does not aim to found a new religion or even another religious sect. It aims rather to bring about more harmonious relationship between the five principle religions of the world and to foster universal brotherhood and world peace by urging people to sink their differences in the tenets of their religious beliefs, their manners and customs, their languages and culture, and their colour and race. Hence it welcomes all people into its membership irrespective of race, colour or creed. It might be called the United Nations of the religious world.

It is also the other object of this Society, namely, to intensify deeds of benevolence by its members, that appeals so much to our people that it has grown so fast and spread so far. Before the war broke out between China and Japan in 1937, the number of branches rose to nearly five hundred in China, over two hundred in Japan and Korea, spreading as far as Singapore and Malaya. Its members are constantly reminded that all good gifts come from God and He expects us to use them for the benefit of mankind as an expression of our love for them. Those possessing wealth should contribute liberally for deeds of benevolence. Others who have talents for organizing and giving works of mercy should make use of their ability. Then all of us should contribute our strength and time to forward the work of the Society.

The deeds of benevolence take on two definite lines. One is of temporary nature, to bring relief whenever and wherever any calamity should fall upon any unfortunate people such as a flood or a great fire or an epidemic of some kind. The Society usually has a trained corps ready for such purpose. Some even maintain two or more corps. It is made up of a corps leader with about twenty workers. A few of them are paid for their services while most of them are volunteers. The reason why the Society spread into Japan was the result of our sending such corps to Yokohama and Tokyo after the great earthquake disaster in 1923. In winter padded clothes are distributed to the needy, especially in North China where it is quite cold in winter, while in South China free tea is provided during the summer months.

In a more or less permanent way, most of these Societies keep a free clinic and a free school. Some of the more wealthy Societies have hospitals and homes for the aged people and maintain several schools in different sections of the city. From these schools workers for the Society are being recruited.

There are of course other forms of social service which should gain the attention of those who are blessed with good health and are fairly well off. We must always remember those who are afflicted with one disease or another or handicapped with the loss of sight or hearing. Tuberculosis, cancer, and leprosy take a big toll on the lives of many of our fellow beings. While we must look to medical science for the final elimination of such afflictions, we should all bear a share in providing them with proper care and medical attention before remedies could be found to cure them or better still to prevent the spread of these dreaded diseases. There is no limit in the scope of social service and it is our inherent duty to do our part in promoting the social welfare of our fellow men.

Chapter 12

The Good Roads Movement

Since my return from America after graduation from Yale University, I was kept so busy with political activities, first in the Revolutionary work and then after the overthrow of the Manchu regime was placed in positions which required my full time and energy, that I had scarcely any time left to do much thinking on other matters, though vital and important as some of them are. I was very much struck with the lack of good roads in China. In my travels in America and Europe I could not help but notice the vast difference between the countries with good roads and others without them. In my spare moments I often raised this question with myself: "why have we no good roads in China?" As I had more time to do some hard thinking on this vital question on my return from the Paris Peace Conference by the end of 1919, when I was rather free from political activities, I resolved to give my full attention to this question until a way should be found to solve it.

The first step I took was to study the effects of good roads on the welfare of our people. I thought this would enable them to travel faster but without cars it would make a little difference in so far as time is concerned. Walking would be a trifle easier on well paved roads but the time saved would be rather negligible. Then again I thought of moving goods faster. But to push a cart over a good road might be a trifle faster than over a dirt road. How could I convince our authorities that good roads would be beneficial to our people? I was almost on the point of giving up the idea of promoting a good roads movement, since I could not convince myself that good roads would be beneficial to our people. Then an idea struck me forcibly. Why not make a survey where good roads existed in China? To my dismay as well as to my great joy I found that goods roads were to be found practically in the foreign concessions only. There were less than a thousand miles in the whole of China then and most of them were in foreign controlled areas. There were other factors of course in bringing prosperity to these areas but I found good roads were a principal factor for their prosperity. There were more people on wide and well-paved roads, as business moved in to such areas, thereby raising the value of prosperity bordering on these roads. As more shops opened up more people would do their shopping there and as more people came to buy things, there would be more shops and the price of land would again go up more. So this circle of prosperity would go on and on indefinitely.

To my dismay because this prosperity would and did enrich the foreign businessmen so much so that neighboring cities and towns would suffer and decline. But this was also to my great joy because I saw that it would be a starting point for us to promote a good roads movement. Accordingly I enlisted the support of one hundred of our leading businessmen, property owners, newspapermen, educators and doctors, and launched the China Good Roads' Association. We engaged a full time General Secretary and a staff of other workers. Pamphlets were prepared to show reasons how good roads attract business, make it easier for children to attend schools, give better health to the people when there is fresh air to breath, and in general bring prosperity to their cities and towns. We made our first appeal to cities like Nanking, Chuikiang, Wusih, Soochow in Kiangsu province and Hangchow, Ningpo, Shaosing, Kasing in Chekiang province. The response was so encouraging that the Board of Directors of the Association decided to publish a Monthly with our energetic General Secretary, Mr. Wu Shan as the Editor. Sample copies of our Monthly were sent to every provincial government. The demand for our magazine was so great that sometimes we had to produce a second edition for the current month. Even from distant provinces like Szechuan, Yunnan and Kansu subscriptions for our Monthly began to pour in. We knew then that many of our people throughout the country felt the needs of having good roads in their cities as we did.

The next step we took was to advocate the building of roads that would connect the different cities. Again we turned our attention to the cities between Shanghai and Nanking and between Shanghai and Hangchow. Some of our Board thought that since travel was relatively easy between these cities, having then already the Shanghai-

Chapter 12   The Good Roads Movement

Nanking and the Shanghai-Hangchow railways, besides the waterways available, this suggestion might fall on deaf ears when presented to the local governments as well as to the two provincial governments of Kiangsu and Chekiang. A careful study showed that there were many cities in this area untapped by the two railways and had no waterways to serve them. The inhabitants in these cities had a most difficult time to reach the railway stations. They had to walk miles to board a train. Goods had to be carried over on the backs or shoulders. They had then a kind of a cart known as the wheelbarrow, with only one wheel in the middle of the cart, as the footpaths were so narrow as not to be able to accommodate two wheels.

Accordingly a plan was drawn up to have these two roads so constructed as not to be running on a parallel line with the railways but in an "S" shape or sometimes a double "S" in order to give facilities to such cities and towns a better means of communications. When presented to the cities and towns concerned and to the two provincial governments, it was met with full approval. The only objection came from cities and towns which were left out in the plan. This gave us the ready answer by pointing out to them that they could build intercity roads to connect them with the main roads.

Although our plan was fully approved and accepted by the various authorities concerned, progress in carrying out the plan was often obstructed by lack of funds to build the roads. We pointed out to them that good roads would inevitably enhance the value of landed property bordering on them, thereby increasing the taxes on such property. The initial expenses could be met by the issue of city bonds or by borrowing from the banks, earmarking the taxes as collaterals. This helped to accelerate the construction work, so that the two contemplated roads were completed as scheduled and the increased taxes came in as expected. The authorities were so pleased with the result that a third road was built to connect Nanking with Hangchow.

The success of this plan had a profound effect on the other cities and provinces. Before long intercity and inter-province roads made their appearance without our urging. Our Association was often called upon to give advice on the planning of the roads and the ways and means to finance their construction.

By the time of the Japanese invasion in 1937, it was estimated that over one hundred thousand miles of roads had been constructed.

Before the launching of the China Good Roads Association less than a thousand miles were in existence and mostly in foreign concessions. It was a great joy and satisfaction to the Association that the Movement was so well backed up by the people and governments. In reviewing the effects which good roads had brought to the country, they seemed to run in all directions. In the first place it facilitated traveling. People could visit places of interest so much more easily and comfortably and at a much less expense. Motorcars, motorcycles, trucks and buses began to appear on these roads, gradually increased in numbers, and took longer journeys as the roads were extended.

Then goods began to move from one province to another in less time and at less cost. Instead of resorting to coolies carrying them and moving at the rate of twenty to thirty miles per day with roads less than one hundred pounds per coolie, now trucks could move them in tons at twenty to thirty miles per hour. Farm products could now reach much wider markets and did not suffer damages as in the old days when several days were needed for their transportation.

The town and cities touched by the roads began to have a much larger volume of business, bringing greater prosperity to the inhabitants. New business sprang up in various forms. The most notable was the establishment of factories in places where the materials for manufactured products were in abundance but formally had no means of getting these products to the markets at a low cost especially of the bulky kind, such as tiles, bricks and earthen utensils.

What benefits the roads bring to the inhabitants of towns and villages are too numerous to be listed, but I must mention one which was a surprise to us all. In talking with the gentry and other leaders in a number of cities in the interior, we were told that since the extension of the roads they could get teachers for their schools. The schools on the coast, particularly those in Shanghai, were turning out then hundreds of graduates every year but they were reluctant to go to these towns to teach on account of the difficulties to get there. It often would take several days or even weeks to do so. But after roads came into existence and with the rapid transit of motorcars and buses, they could get there in a few hours and at most in a day or two.

The Japanese invasion disrupted the functioning of our Association in that our Board and our staff of workers were scattered all over the country, but, strange as it may sound, the invasion brought about an

Chapter 12 The Good Roads Movement

acceleration in the construction of roads. The coastal provinces, although stood much in need of good roads, are fortunate to have many waterways. The great Yangtze and Pearl Rivers have many and long tributaries. Besides, there were already constructed two trunk lines of railways, connecting north China with south China. But the vast hinterland provinces were denied of both railways and waterways. Our Central Government had to move to Chungking. Although it had easy access to the sea over the Yangtze River, it was blocked from Hankow eastward. To meet the situation our National Government took upon itsself to build national roads from Kansu in the northwest to Yunnan in the southwest, a distance of approximately 5000 miles. The hinterland provinces also undertook to build roads to join up with the national roads. By the time when our National Government was back in Nanking in 1945, we had approximately over 200,000 miles of roads constructed.

While it is true that our roads could not yet be compared with those in Europe or America, either in quality or length, yet a beginning has been made. From the start the Good Roads Association did not advocate for expensive and well built roads at the beginning so as not to overtax either the Central Government or the Provincial and Local Governments. As traffic begins to increase, as it is bound to do in due course of time, more taxes will be derived. Therefrom, these roads could be further improved and increased. I would not propose to revive our old Good Roads Association. It has done its part in promoting the idea. It is up to the nation now to see to it that the roads are well kept, improved and increased to bring greater prosperity to our people.

Chapter 13

The Shantung Question

When the Chinese Delegation refused to sign the Paris Peace Treaty with Germany, the final disposition of the Shantung question remained unsettled. The Peace Conference agreed to hand over all the German rights in Shantung to Japan, which the Chinese Delegation absolutely and resolutely opposed. We were in the right. Japan could not claim them as the spoils of war, for China and Japan were not at war. In fact we were both allies fighting against Germany our common enemy. The sympathy of the whole world was on China's side. Even Japan had to acknowledge that these Shantung rights should be returned to the lawful owner, in that she accepted an invitation from the United States for China and Japan to reopen the question in Washington with America as mediator.

Dr. W. W. Yen was then our Foreign Minister and he appointed Dr. Wang Ching-hui, Dr. Alfred Shao-ki Sze and Dr. V. K. Wellington Koo as our delegates to the Washington meeting. I was asked to look after the negotiations at the home end. Because of our inherent rights and in face of the world opinions in our favour, the Japanese government finally signed an accord with us agreeing to return all the German rights in Shantung to China. As these rights were so varied that further negotiations would be required on the details with, however, a time limit that they must be completed by the end of that year. The accord was signed in Washington on _____ [sic] 1922.

I was then appointed Director-General for these negotiations with the Governor of Shantung Gen. Tien Chung-yu, as my Associate. Although he was a military man by training, he was quite a good Chinese scholar and a man of tact and wisdom. He left to my judgment in the settlement of the various questions involved and gave me full support when the time came to take over the Tsingtao-Tsinan railway, the various coal mines, the vast salt fields, and finally the port of Tsingtao.

I set up my office in Peking so as to be in close touch with our Foreign Office. The Japanese government had appointed Mr. Obata, the then Japanese Minister in Peking to be my opposite member. Steps were immediately taken to find the right persons to assist me in the discharge of this duty, not only to have all the questions ironed out in the negotiations with the Japanese representatives, but, after an agreement was arrived at, also to take over the numerous enterprises, installations, buildings and other properties, started by the Germans towards the end of the last century to the time they were wrested from them by the Japanese and subsequent improvements made by the Japanese in the seven years of their occupation. In looking back to that eventful year, I feel I was most fortunate to have had such a splendid body of men to assist me. They ware men who knew the importance of bringing the negotiations to a satisfactory conclusion and of taking over the many-sided enterprises without any interruption or derangement. They ware well experienced in their different lines of work, railway administration, civil and mechanical engineering, railway maintenance, mining administration and mining engineering, salt industry, city administration, harbour control, police patrol on land and water and one hundred and one other matters. My object was to demonstrate to the world that our people were capable of taking care of these enterprises. I had in mind of persuading eventually those foreign powers which had wrenched from the weak-kneed and ignorant Manchu regime, such concessions, settlements and other rights, to return them to China. In other words China must recover every sovereign right lost to us since the opening of the country to foreign trade over a century ago. This I finally succeeded to do during the fourth term of my office in Foreign Affairs. More will be said in subsequent chapters.

Mr. Obara and I started our negotiations with only one session a day. We went over our subjects one by one. Any subject for which we could not find a solution would be set aside for further discussions. In that way they were gradually narrowed down but there were several thorny ones that could not be ironed out even after many sessions. Since there was a deadline to our negotiations, we agreed to meet twice a day and eventually we had to have three sessions a day, one in the morning, one in the afternoon, and one in the evening. Some of the evening sessions were carried on as late as midnight.

The overall principle of our negotiations was that all the expenditures the Germans had incurred in the construction of railways, mines, salt fields, government buildings and other properties, would be automatically reverted to China as her assets, but expenditures incurred by the Japanese in the way of improvements and extensions during her occupation would be compensated for by China. This required careful study and investigation on our part to see that the claims for such improvements and extensions were justified by facts. I must state here that the Japanese did put in a lot of improvements on the various enterprises started by the Germans, and in some cases a good deal of extensions, particularly the salt fields. The Tsingtao harbour and its adjacent beaches were especially fitted for salt fields and Japan was in great need of salt to supplement her own production.

The chief fault of the Japanese estimates was due to the fact that they were taken at the current value, which would be certainly much higher than what had been actually spent when the improvements and/or extensions were made. So we had to scrutinize their figures carefully by checking over their books. Eventually, practically all the questions were settled satisfactorily to both parties. There was a good deal of shoptalks, bargaining over the amounts. I will mention just one of such bargaining. Most of the salt fields were put in by the Japanese, so it was up to us to compensate for them. The estimate put up by the Japanese was around $11,000,000 (Chinese currency). After careful investigation we found that actual expenses incurred by Japan was (were) only about $4,000,000. At the session when this question was first brought up for discussion, I countered with an offer of $2,000,000. Of course I knew Mr. Obata could not accept my counter offer. This thorny question was brought up time and again but we could not agree on an amount satisfactory to both parties, although Mr. Obata gradually brought the estimates down to $9,000,000 and finally to $7,000,000. I stood put on my offer — almost towards the end of our negotiations. We had only a few questions left of which the salt question was the most difficult one. I saw that Mr. Obata was most anxious to have this matter settled once for all. He made a remark that he would lose his head should he agree to any amount less than $7,000,000, jokingly patting his neck. I countered by patting my own neck and said that I would agree to $4,000.000, using a sort of take-it-or leave it attitude. To my surprise he said he would take it even at the risk of losing his head and I said I would risk my head by doubling my offer. I was roundly censored by a section of our own people for making such a poor bargain by doubling the amount at one jump. I succeeded in quieting them by calling their representatives in for a conference when I showed to them the real value of the salt fields from an authoritative source. I was further justified when these fields were later auctioned off for $7,000,000 — to the Salt merchants! The amount asked by the Japanese was based on current prices which I declined to accept, but the amount I agreed to pay was a trifle better than what was actually spent on them. The successful conclusion of our negotiations was based on give and take. Both Mr. Obata and I proved to be good compromisers. We just managed to conclude our negotiations successfully on that basis and on time. His work was now over but mine was only half done. I had to see to it that everything was to be taken over without a hitch.

During the negotiations I had to visit Shantung quite frequency in order to get first hand information on the various questions concerned but particularly to consult Governor Tien on the necessary steps to be taken when we were to take over the numerous interests spread over the province. Our first concern was to protect the railway properties running from one end of the province to the other. A Special Corps of railway guards had to be formed. Most of the men were drawn from the ranks of the army with policy officers under our able Policy Commissioner, Mr. Cheng Sung-shan. Governor Tien also had soldiers distributed in the important centres, so that in case of emergency they could be called upon to assist the guards. Fortunately, these soldiers were never called upon as the handing over of the whole railway line was completed according to schedule without any hitch. Movements of trains continued regularly. The only difference the travelers noticed was that in place of Japanese guards they now had their own countrymen to give them protection.

The taking over of the coal mines was effected much more easily, as they were centred in two areas connected with the main railway line with branch lines. These mines furnished coal for the locomotives and factories, besides a fairly large balance for export through Tsingtao to Shanghai and over the Tientsin-Pukow railway to meet the demands for coal along the Yangtze river. Some of the Japanese technicians were still retrained but the mines were fully protected by our own police and military guards and were in control of the men we had chosen to manage them. Other properties connected either with the railway or the mines were also taken over smoothly.

Finally, we had to tackle the much more complicated task to take over the administration of the port of Tsingtao. I was appointed head of the administration with the high title of Governor of Tsingtao. It was really a misnomer. The proper title should have been simply Mayor of Tsingtao. Usually, only the head of a provincial government was given the title of Governor. However, the Central Government in conferring this title on me had considered the fact that the Germans and the Japanese had always a Governor for Tsingtao and further Governor Tien was my associate in our negotiations with the Japanese. To give me the title of mayor would be construed as a demotion. The Central Government wanted to reward me for the successful handling of the negotiations. To me it was immaterial by what title I should be addressed. The important task before me was to take over the administration as smoothly as the railways, mines and other accessory properties.

Accordingly, accompanied by my personal staff, I went to Tsingtao a few days ahead of the day fixed for the handing over of the administration to us. Most of my associates who were to share with me the burden of the administration were already in Tsingtao for some time, in order to get acquainted with the local situation. Many of them had been with me during our negotiations and I must mention the name of Dr. H. H. Kung, my old friend and fellow worker on so many fields of activities. He was most helpful in my negotiations with the Japanese and agreed to continue his association with me in order to complete our common task to get back our lost rights for the country.

The ceremony of officially handing over the City and Port of Tsingtao by the Japanese Governor, Gen. _____ [sic], took place at the Government House known as the Chung Tu Fu. It was a stately building, erected by the Germans and well maintained by the Japanese. Besides being the official residence of the Governor and his family, it had a [sic] large-sized halls for banquets and other official functions, besides offices for the higher ranking officials. After the ceremony was over I spent the day in supervising the smooth working of the various organs of the City government. I was always on the

Chapter 13 The Shantung Question

alert to see that the city was well protected. There was a good deal of banditry in Shantung. I was afraid that some of these gangs might filtrate into the port during the changeover of the administration. So I specially instructed the Police Commissioner to inform me immediately, if he should find any indication of their activities.

Nothing happened during the day, but towards the evening I received a message from the Commissioner that in Li-Ts'un, a village some five miles from the city, some suspicious characters were collecting into small bands. Besides instructing him to have sufficient police force on the spot, I drove over to that village with a bodyguard in another car following mine. The report added that a notorious bandit chief by the name of Sun Tien-ying was there. We drove around the village and saw everything was quiet, so we returned to the city. Again another report came that Sun Tien-ying was in a certain hotel in the city. Immediately I set out for that hotel. I did not want to arrest him or any other person merely on suspicion. I was sure that a personal visit by me would turn the trick. When he was pointed out to me as the man by that name, I purposely raised my voice, as if addressing the people gathering around me but actually with no particular person in mind, and appealed to them to help the government to maintain peace and order on patriotic grounds. Whether it was due to that personal appeal or not, nothing untoward happened that evening either. Before I retired that night I offered a fervent prayer of thanksgiving to the Good Lord for His inspiration and guidance to enable me to discharge my duties faithfully and courageously. I knew that if the first day could be passed peacefully, then the situation would be well in hand. I must give credit to our own people for their loyal co-operation and also to the large number of Japanese residents in Tsingtao whose behavior was so splendid.

I was looking forward to a long term of office as the Mayor of Tsingtao in spite of the high sounding title of Governor given to me by the National Government. I was conscious of the good staff I had in the administration of the city and in the excellent support from our people not only in Tsingtao but throughout the country. The leader of our Revolutionary Movement, Dr. Sun Yat-sen, for whom I had my greatest respect, gave me all the encouragement to carry on my work. But there was a political crisis in Peking and a new Premier was appointed and I was asked to join his cabinet as the Foreign Minister.

But for my loyalty to an old friend, Mr. Wang Ta-hsieh, who was to be the next Premier and for the fact that I was always working for the recovery of our rights, I would not have accepted the offer. I thought that it was my duty to assume the post in order to carry out my lifelong aim to make my country a full sovereign state among the family of nations. I had to spend the next few days in winding up my affairs, both personal and official, and to hand over the administration to my successor, Mr. Yang.

I was somewhat troubled over this turnover for I was not sure that my successor had enough training and experience to handle the affairs of a modern city. I had several conferences with the heads of the various departments of the city government and urged them to carry on their work as if I were still the Governor. Although my sizing-up of the capacity of my successor was correct, as he proved to be quite ignorant as to how a modern city should be administered, he let the departmental heads carrying on their work without interruption. Before I was able to leave Tsingtao I was notified by the National Government that I had, in addition to the post of Foreign Minister, also to act as the Premier, as Mr. Wang Ta-hsieh had handed in his resignation as Premier due to the opposition from certain political parties against him. So I left Tsingtao with a puzzled and somewhat an uneasy mind.

Chapter 14

In Troubled Waters

After the unsuccessful attempt of Yuan Shih-k'ai to set up a monarchy with himself as the founder of a new dynasty and followed by his death immediately thereafter, the country had been badly torn up politically. The general who commanded the largest force was able to get himself appointed by hook or crook, Tu-chun or War Lord of a province. Some of these War Lords ruled over more than one province. Notable among them was General Chan Tso-lin who started his life as a bandit and rose to rule over the province of Fengtien. In a surprisingly short time his power extended to the other two provinces adjacent to it, in an area larger than Germany. This area was once the home of the Manchus, hence it was often referred to as Manchuria. It was separated from China Proper by the Great Wall built by Emperor Chin Shih-huang before the Christian era. Outside of this Great Wall lived the hordes of nomads, generally known as Tartars, but consisted of many different tribes, the most well-known among them being the Leads, the Chins, the Mongols and the Manchus. But by the time when Gen. Chang Tso-lin was Tu-chun of the Three Eastern Provinces, the Chinese name for Manchuria, I believe there were less than a million genuine Manchus living in these three provinces. The bulk of the population of over ten millions consisted of sturdy formers from Shantung, Shansi and Hopei. The last named province was formerly and also better known as Chihli, the Metropolitan province, because the National Capital, Peking, was located in this province.

Although Yuan Shih-k'ai was dead, the powerful cohorts, which he had raised and trained under German tutors and equipped with modern arms, still existed. Most of the men composing this modern army came from the province of Chihli. They were strongly entrenched inside of the Great Wall. Moreover, they had strong satellites in the rich provinces along the Yangtze river and the eastern coast. They also had the advantage of being in control of the National Government. The existence of these two powerful factions side by side and only with the Great Wall separating them could not but anger for a final conflict. I have already alluded to the "war" between Gen. Wu Pei-fu, who then represented the Chihli faction, and Gen. Chang Tso-lin of the Fengtien faction. I will again refer to it later in this chapter.

When Dr. Sun Yat-sen was convinced that the men surrounding Yuan Shih-k'ai after the latter's betrayal could not be trusted to build up a strong and unified China, he took steps soon thereafter to have a true Republican government set up with Canton as the headquarters. Supported by the Chinese navy and the leaders of the National Assembly and veteran statesmen like Mr. Tong Shao-yi and Dr. Wu Ting-fang, this government came into being just soon after the first World War started. In order to put up a united front in so far as foreign relations were concerned, the policy of his government generally known to the outside world as the "Southern" government was to work in with the "Northern" government as the Peking regime was nicknamed. It was the carrying out of this policy that I consented to represent China at the Paris Peace Conference and with the full blessing of Dr. Sun. We did not sign our Peace Treaty with Germany in Paris. It was due to our refusal to recognize the clauses awarding the German rights in Shantung to Japan. These rights rightly and inherently belong to China. I had no quibble in my conscience when undertaking these two tasks, difficult and strenuous as they were. But to be appointed as the Foreign Minister of the "Northern" government and coupled with the duties of its Premier, did make me feel uneasy. After prayerful consideration and with the advice of my best friends, I decided to accept the appointments but with a clear premonition that I was sailing into troubled waters.

Peking was then the centre of political maneuvers and intrigues. Rival factions fought with one another for the control of the central government, although its authority was reduced to such a low scale so that it was seldom respected beyond its walls! After the death of President Yuan Shih-k'ai, Vice-President Li Yuan-hung assumed the office of the President. But hardly was he able even to warm the seat of the Chief Magistrate, an upstart in the person of General Chang Hsün made an attempt to pull off a coup-d'état by marching his

Chapter 14 In Troubled Waters

forces to the National Capital with the avowed purpose of reseating the abdicated boy Emperor Hsüan T'ung on the throne. It was a puerile gesture, so contrary to the wishes of our people. The timely and energetic steps taken by General Tuan Chi-jui quashed Chang Hsün's forces in a short skirmish, not even to be dignified with the name of a battle. There was no response to Chang Hsün's stupid appeal what so ever.

President Li Yuan-hung was back at the capital again. I had a great deal of respect for President Li Yuan-hung as a man. He was loyal and faithful to the cause of the Republic. I often wished that we had a chief executive who had the ability of Yuan Shih-k'ai and the integrity of Li Yuan-hung. China then could have made much greater progress. Unfortunately, President Li Yuan-hung was lacking in ability to accomplish what he wanted to, especially in a period of factional strife, both militarily and politically. He was unable even to pacify the two warring factions between Chihli and Fenghtien at the very door of the National Capital. So the country remained hopelessly disordered to the end of his administration. One political crisis after another was the order of the day and cabinets changed as often as there was a crisis. General Feng Kuo-chang was elected the next President but he fumbled at the political game as badly as his predecessor. He was in the office of the Chief Executive only for a short period when death removed him from it.

The next President, Mr. Hsu Shih-ch'ang was far more experienced in government administrations, having been in high government positions during the Manchu regime. At one time he was Governor-General of the Three Eastern Provinces. His elevation to the presidency gave better promises to unify country, but the warring factions still proved too much for him to overcome. Finding that he was unable to bring cooperation between Gen. Wu Pei-fu and Gen. Chang Tso-lin, he quietly left the Capital for his home in Tientsin and handed in his resignation from his office. The immediate result was an open conflict between the two generals when Wu Pei-fu was definitely defeated on the field of battle.

There was some fear that Chang Tso-lin might pull off a trick to set up the Manchu ex-Emperor again. The Japanese had been hobnobbing with him and had given him much support, financially at least, in the fight between him and Wu Pei-fu. Although Wu was defeated, his patriotism and stand for an independent China found much sympathy among the nation at large. General Tuan Chi-jui came out once more for the defence of the Republic. He made it clear that he would rally all the forces available to maintain the Republic. His stand received a nationwide support which must have clashed any hope of revising the monarchy. There was of curse no overt act or declaration on the part of Chang Tso-lin but his acquiescence to accept the new regime in Parking with General Tuan as Chief Executive ad interim was a clear indication of his understanding of the sentiment prevailing all over the country. The Japanese would have wished so much to see that the Manchu ex-Emperor was put on the throne again. At that time Hsüan T'ung, the abdicated boy-Emperor, was living in the Japanese concession in Tientsin. Subsequent events proved what the Japanese jingoes would have done had an attempt been made to revive the monarchy after the victory of Chang Tso-lin over Wu Pei-fu. When Japan actually started war with China in 1937, Hsüan T'ung was put up as the Emperor of a puppet empire, known as Manchu Kuo. It was alleged that Chang Tso-lin's refusal to revive the monarchy had caused his death when a bomb exploded under his carriage while traveling on the Manchurian railway near Mukden as Fengtien was generally known to the Western world. Be that as it may, Chang Tso-lin's acquiescence prolonged the life of the Republic, although the country was still as divided as ever since Yuan Shih-k'ai's death.

When I accepted the position of the Foreign Minister and later also the duties of the Acting Premier, I was fully conscious that I was to sail into troubled waters. My sole motive was to carry out Dr. Sun's declared foreign policy to revise the unequal treaties with the nations of the world. In so far as this policy was concerned, both the "southern" and the "northern" governments were in full accord, starting with our delegation to the Paris Peace Conference, throughout our negotiations with the Japanese and the final return of German rights in Shantung to us. The fact that the "northern" government would ask me to head its Foreign Office showed that it shared with the "southern" government the aspiration of the whole nation to regain our full sovereignty through the revision of these unequal treaties. Accordingly, soon after my assumption of the Foreign Office, I made an official declaration with the approval of the cabinet to that effect. The chancelleries of the world, particularly those of the leading Powers, took my declaration as a bomb shell. They brought so much diplomatic pressure to bear upon the President, who failed to see the importance of such a move on China's past, that he felt that the best way out was to have a new cabinet appointed. So I was out. That was the shortest time I served my country as its Foreign Minister for the first time.

However, there was wide spread support for the stand I took. The next year when another cabinet was installed I was again asked to head the Foreign Office with General Huang Fu as the Premier. As Mr. Chow Tso-min, a very well-known financier, having been General Manager of the King-cheng Banking Corporation for many years declined to serve as the Finance Minister on account of his business connections, I was asked to act concurrently for that office also. I did not feel that I was the right person to look after this arm of the government, but I was prevailed upon to take it temporarily until another suitable person could be found. That ministry, I found to my great relief, was quiet well staffed with experienced men, so I asked them to carry on their routine work without referring to me. I had only a couple of secretaries appointed to serve as my eyes and ears. I concentrated my attentions on the work of the Foreign Office. The first thing I did in assuming my office as Foreign Minister for the second time was to repeat my declaration that the unequal treaties which China had entered into with the other nations of the world must be overhauled. It was received with better grace by the various capitals. I believe that with the first shock over, they were prepared to get a second shot in their arms. China had certainly a good case asking for a revision of these treaties. Conditions had definitely changed since the establishment of the Republic. China merely wanted to deal with the other nations on an equal and fair basis. Still, opposition to revision was quite strong especially from the foreign nationals who had lived in China and been fattened from these unequal treaties. They were nicknamed as the "die-hards." Their influence with their respective governments was strong enough so as to bring further diplomatic pressure to have our cabinet ousted. My second tenure of office in the Foreign Ministry lasted seven months, much longer than my first, but the inevitable thing happened. There was to be another cabinet to take over our work and I was appointed Director-General of a

Commission to carry on negotiations with Russia. I thought it was a graceful way to keep me out of the Foreign Office, due no doubt to the subtle pressure that was brought to bear on our Chief Executive by the "die-hards" in China through their diplomatic agents.

In my second administration of the Foreign Office, through the time was still too short accomplish much, I succeeded in doing two things. One was to lay the foundation for the calling of a Tariff Convention and the other was to start negotiations for a new treaty with the Union of Soviet Socialist Republic.

Since the opening of China to foreign trade, those in power then were so ignorant about tariff matters that our customs only levied a flat 5% ad valorem duty on all goods imported to or exported from China irrespective of their kind or quality. We could not change our tariff rates without the unanimous consent of the foreign governments of the countries having trade with China. While other nations could raise or lower their tariff rates on various articles to meet trade conditions whether to encourage, discourage, or prohibit such imports or exports, China was iron-bound to a flat rate on all articles. At the Paris Peace Conference this question was among others raised by China for examination and readjustment. Our object then was merely to voice the injustice that was being done to her in denying her tariff autonomy.

I started out my campaign by talking individually and separately with the ministers of those countries having fairy large volumes of trade with us. Having ascertained their views on the question, I arranged for a Round Table Conference at the Foreign Office and presented to them the justice of our case and called for their support. I had them seated in such a way so that when I called upon them individually to express their views, I would have those in our favour speak up first. Mr. Oudendyck (?) [sic] the Dutch Minister, being Doyen of the diplomatic body, was the first one to be called upon. I knew that he was very much in favour of according tariff autonomy to us as one of the inherent rights of an independent nation. He was followed by the Danish, the Japanese, the American and other ministers who all spoke in support of our case. The British minister was among the last to be called upon for I knew it would be difficult for him to speak his own mind. Among the "die-hards" in China, the British had the largest number. Had he been asked to speak among the first, he

Chapter 14 In Troubled Waters

might have compromised the question by expressing some doubt as to whether it would be the right time to make the change or something to that effect. I noticed that he was at a loss to know what to say when his turn came to be called upon. He must have opened his mouth two or three times before words came out of his lips. Finally, he simply said that since there was unanimous agreement among his colleagues, he would also stand by it. I clinched the situation by thanking all of them for their favourable support. This Round Table Conference laid the foundation for a Tariff Convention held a year later when I became Foreign Minister for the third time.

Our relation with Russia had bought many losses to China. After the termination of the Yuan dynasty, the Ming Emperors succeeded in pacifying the once all-powerful Mongols and the Chinese Empire extended to the wilds of Siberia. During the Ch'ing dynasty the Russians continued to make inroads into the Chinese territory, till her influence was felt in the Three Eastern Provinces and Korea. Towards the end of the last century, when the danger of the "Partition of China" was at its height, Russia had wrenched important concessions from China. Port Arthur and Darien, two superb ice-free ports, together with the rights of building a railway connecting Siberia with these ports, were among the concessions China had agreed to grant to Russia. The overthrow of the Czarist regime by the Russian revolution paved the way for Lenin and Trosky [Trotsky] to grab the supreme power of government from Kerensky who was heading the revolutionary movement. After they had firmly established their power over the whole of Russia, they wanted to gain the friendship of China by publicly declaring that whatever concessions the Czars had obtained from China would be returned to her. Mr. Yurin was first sent to Peking and later replaced by Mr. Joffre (?) [Joffe] [sic] but there was no response from China. At the successful conclusion of our negotiations with Japan over the German rights in Shantung, I was able to convince our government leaders that we should and could negotiate with Russia for the return of their rights to us. That was one of the reasons why I was chosen to head the Sino-Russian negotiations.

Mr. Karakhan was then the Russian representative in Peking and soon after my appointment arrangements were made for our negotiations to get started. Besides setting up an office, I had to find the right personnel to assist me. Most of my former associates were left in

115

Tsingtao. Moreover, I had to find a number of assistants who understood the new problems we had to handle and to be able to speak Russian. I found Mr. Karakhan a rather pleasant man to work with. His English was rather limited and I knew nothing of the Russian language. So our negotiations required more time. Everything said by either side had to be interpreted.

After several sessions of our negotiations, it was quite evident to me that the Russians wanted to retract on quite a number of points from their formal declaration, the most important ones being the railway rights and the status of Outer Mongolia. I will not burden my readers with the details of our negotiations. To make the long story short I will merely state that I succeeded in keeping the Russians to live up to their declaration which I insisted formed the basis of our negotiations. The only important point that I agreed to acknowledge and concede was over some of the railway rights. At one point the negotiations were nearly on the point of a complete breakdown. I insisted at first that the railway rights should be reverted to China without any compensation in accordance with the declaration made by Russia. However I tried to ease the situation by agreeing to a fifty-fifty ownership of the railways for ____ [sic] years at the end of which all the railway rights should be turned over to China. I stipulated though that during these years the management should be under a Chinese Director-General with the heads of the departments equally divided between Chinese and Russian nationals. I took care that the heads of the traffic, finance and police departments be held by Chinese. It took many sessions for this question to be thrashed out before it was finally agreed to by both sides.

Another knotty question was the status of Outer Mongolia. I insisted that China must have sovereignty over that area as over any other part of the country. Russia wanted China only to have suzerainty over it. We had spent many hours on the question. We could not come to an agreement on it even towards the end of our negotiations. The last session took us till the wee hours of the next day. Mr. Karakhan stated that his English was not sufficient to differentiate these two words and wanted to have the standard dictionary for him to get a clear idea what the difference was between them. I was convinced in my own mind that he was merely stalling for time to get his final instruction from Moscow. So I played up to him. I instructed my secretary to borrow a copy of that dictionary from the Peking National Library. We knew the Library would be closed by that late hour, so my secretary understood when I told him to go to the librarian's home to get the latter out of bed, if necessary, in order to let us have the dictionary. It took him a long time to get it but finally that section of the dictionary containing all the 3 [sic] words beginning with an "S" was brought to our meeting place. I let Mr. Karakhan to have all the time he wanted to make a thorough study of these two "strange" words. This was one of the days when I consumed more than ten cigars, in order to while away the time and keep me awake. Incidentally I wish to point out that the habit of cigar smoking is good for a diplomat. Not only it stimulates his mind, but also when he has a difficult question to answer requiring time to do a little thinking, that is the moment to thrust the cigar into his mouth and evidently to show his appreciation of smoking by sucking at it hard and long!

At long last, almost at dawn, Mr. Karakhan returned to the room, where the session was being held, with an expression on his face indicating his full understanding of the difference between "Sovereignty" and "Suzerainty." I gave a signal to my secretary to have champagne ready. As soon as he informed me through his interpreter that he would agree with me to use the word "Sovereignty" on the new accord, I stood up and asked him to join with me to celebrate the success of our negotiations by drinking champagne together. It must have been a surprise to him that at that instant a tray of champagne glasses was brought in together with two bottles of the best brand. Even our secretaries and interpreters shared with us over the successful conclusion of our rather prolonged negotiations.

The factional fight was still going on fiercely in the capital but I took care not to take part in the political maneuvers and stuck to my own work in order to ensure successful conclusion of my negotiations with Mr. Karakhan. Even here a nasty situation came up when Fengtien insisted the Sino-Russian accord should also be signed by them, in spite of the fact that I had quite a number of the Fengtien faction on my commission and that in diplomatic practice only the Central Government could sign any treaty with a foreign government representative. To satisfy Gen. Chang Tso-lin and to make it easy to carry out the terms of the agreement, a similar accord with slight modifications was signed between Mr. Karakhan and the Fengtien representative. I made a personal visit to the Three Eastern Provinces when the time came for us to take over the two ports of Port Arthur and Dairen together with the long railway line linking these ports to the Russian borders.

The next year I was appointed Foreign Minister for the third time. My tenure of office this time was longer than my other two terms but it was not long enough for me to carry out what I had twice declared to do. The Customs Convention was held and successfully concluded with the foundation I had laid during my second term of office. This ensured China to exercise her tariff autonomy from then on. I was aware that China's internal political situation was as unstable as ever, so took every precaution to safeguard her relations with the other nations and to carry out Dr. Sun's foreign policy of revising the unequal treaties. With that in view I sought every opportunity to raise our status as an independent nation. I pulled every string I knew to convince the Western powers that China should have a status on an equal footing with them. Before we could have the unequal treaties revised, I tried every convincing argument that China should exchange diplomatic representatives of the Ambassadorial rank. My presentation, however, fell on deaf ears.

One day while I was receiving Minister Karakhan, his rank having been changed to Minister Plenipotentiary and Envoy Extraordinary from a mere representative of a foreign government before the conclusion of the Sino-Russian negotiations, an idea came to my mind that I might succeed in persuading the other Powers, should China and Russia raise their mutual Legations to Embassies first. Accordingly, I made this suggestion to him and he agreed to wire Moscow for instructions. Several days later he paid me another visit when he informed me that Russia would be much pleased to exchange Ambassadors with China. This was so arranged with the first Chinese Ambassador ever stationed in a foreign country, while Russia was the only foreign country in China with a representative of the Ambassadorial rank. This must have piqued the chancelleries of the so-called Great Powers. I took every opportunity to remind the Ministers of the other countries that they would be treated in the usual diplomatic usage when being received by the Foreign Minister. A good opportunity presented itself when I was receiving all the envoys on our Double Ten anniversary that year. I received first the

Chapter 14　In Troubled Waters

only Ambassador in China, namely, Mr. Karakhan. I purposely kept up our conversation much longer than the usual perfunctory visit while keeping all the ministers waiting in the reception room. After keeping them waiting long enough, I raised my glass to drink to the prosperity of Russia while in return he drank to that of China. Then he left me, and I called in all the other ministers together and exchanged toasts with them. This must have made a deep impression on them. This, I consider, must have paved the way for my eventual success in revising the unequal treaties with all the other nations when I was Foreign Minister during my fourth term between 1928-1931, and the raise of Legations to Embassies in the important countries of the world.

In all these years I had been sailing in troubled waters. After the election of Gen. Tsao K'un as the next President, I felt that frequent political crisis was not conducive to the carrying out of a definite foreign policy. Taking advantage of an appointment as the Director of the Lunghai railway, a line that was destined to be the first line of railways running east and west across the country, I moved down to live at Chengchow, the headquarters of the railways. Chengchow is the point where two lines cut across each other, the Lunghai running east and west and the Peking-Hankow line running north and south. There I waited for a better opportunity to fullfil my mission to bring about diplomatic equality between China and the nations of the world.

Chapter 15

The Northern Expedition

I was in a rather low spirit when I left Peking by the beginning of 1926 to assume my new post as the Director-General of the Lunghai railway. I had entertained high hopes when we succeeded in getting back our rights in Shantung after our strenuous fight for them at the Paris Peace Conference and with the conclusion of our negotiations with Japan. I was conscious that the petty warlords in Peking had only their personal gains to consider but had hoped that with a united front on foreign affairs they would sink their personal interests and work for the unity of the country. Among the military leaders in north China, the man for whom I had much respect and from whom much was expected to lead our country out of chaos to unity, was General Tuan Chi-jui. Twice he had warded off the danger of a revival of the Manchu regime. Dr. Sun, I believe, had entertained the same hopes which must have prompted his efforts to bring about an accord between the two warring factions of Chili and Fengtien by a personal visit to Peking in 1924. Unfortunately, death intervened. He was suffering from cancer in the kidney. The Peking Union Medical College Hospital, where he went for treatment, could not save his life, for it was found that no operation could stop its fatal effect.

On his death bed he dictated his famous will in which he stated that for forty years he had given his life to bring about the revolution with a view of accomplishing freedom and equality for his country. From his forty years of experience it was self-evident that to achieve its consummation it was necessary to call the attention of the whole nation and to co-operate with other nations which would accord to us equal treatment. Since the revolution had not yet achieved its purpose, he urged his followers to redouble their efforts by carrying out the principles he had laid down for the reconstruction of China and the methods appertaining thereto, the doctrine of the Three Peoples,

Chapter 15 The Northern Expedition

namely, Peoples' Autonomy, Peoples' Livelihood and Peoples' Rights, and the decisions of the first National Representative Convention. He urged further that in the nearest future a meeting of the Peoples' Convention should be called and efforts be made to terminate the unequal treaties.

Here now is a gist of his will. Anyone could see what was uppermost in his mind, when he was on the point of leaving this world in the physical sense — as one who believed absolutely in what he believed in and knew how he spent the best part of his life to realize his aim in life, his death made me work harder than ever before along the line I was best fitted for to achieve that objective, namely, to put an end to the unequal treaties. Hence every time when I was appointed to the Foreign Office I made the revision of the unequal treaties as the main object of my work. I was only able to make a public declaration during my first term as Foreign Minister and then my work was ended, as the government had appointed another cabinet. During my second term I was able to do slightly more. Besides repeating my public declaration, I succeeded in lining up the nations having treaty with us to agree to call for a Tariff Convention with a view of restoring tariff autonomy to China. Then I was out of the Foreign Office again. It was during my third term when China recovered her tariff autonomy, thereby ended the unequal treatment on tariff. I was hoping that I could start tackling the other parts of our unequal treaties, but another political crisis put an end to my efforts. I was convinced that unless we could have a more stable central government, no efforts on my part would have succeeded in bringing about a termination of our unequal treaties. The election of General Tsao K'un as the next President had made it abundantly clear that there was no hope whatever to carry out the last part of Dr. Sun's will. Tsao K'un was less able but more fickle than any of his predecessors. General Tuan Chi-jiu, the man on whom we had pinned more hopes, was left out by the National Assembly, although he had shown greater ability and more stability as the Chief Executive pro tem after President Hsu Shih Ch'ang resigned from his office.

There was another military leader in north China whom we wanted to win over to support the Republican cause in the person of General Feng Yü-hsiang, often called the Christian General. I came to know him quite well since the time when I was acting President of the

Senate. He came to attend a bible class at my home. After a few months of intensive study of the Bible, he was convinced that in the Christian teachings there was the dynamic power not only to regenerate an individual but also to lead a whole nation to a higher level of civilization, in that men and women would strive harder to lead purer lives and make greater personal sacrifices for their common welfare. In due course, he embraced the Christian faith by being formally baptized and he was an ardent Christian worker both in the army and civilian community. He was then stationed in Loyang in the province of Honan which was once the national capital in the Tang dynasty. I was certainly disappointed over the political situation when I left Peking for my new duties at Chengchow but I was looking forward with anticipation to meeting with my old friend, the "Christian General" again, as Loyang was an important station of the line and not far from Chengchow. We exchanged visits quite often and had long discussions over the various questions we were both interested in. Our chief topic was on the political situation. I informed him confidentially what was in the mind of Dr. Sun and the reason for his visit to Peking. He pledged his full support to the Northern Expedition when it should reach the Yellow river basin.

I have alluded to the founding of a War College at Whampoa under General Chiang Kai-shek. The object of founding this College was to train officers for a new army in order to sweep away the "War Lords" from the country who had no other aim but to fatten themselves at the expense of the people. By 1926 several Divisions were ready to take to the field and the Northern Expedition began to take shape. The first step was to consolidate the base of operation by bringing the two provinces of Kwangtung and Kwangsi under full control of the Central authority. It then extended its control over the neighbouring provinces of Kiangsi and Fukien, and gradually fought its way towards the Yangtze river basin. By 1928 the Expedition had swept up to the Yellow river provinces and the "Christian General," faithful to his pledge, was ready to bring all the forces under him to the support of the "march northward movement." Meanwhile a full fledged Central Government was established in Nanking with Mr. Lin Shen as the President of the Republic and Mr. Tan Yen-k'ai as the Premier. General Chiang Kai-shek was given the title of Generalissimo of the Northern Expedition. An arrangement was made for the two generals

Chapter 15   The Northern Expedition

to meet in Chengchow and I was instrumental in bringing the two together. My good friend Dr. H. H. Kung and several others representing the South had come to Loyang a few months earlier and we had thoroughly prepared the ground for active cooperation in the march towards Peking. After the meeting at Chengchow the Generalissimo continued his journey towards Tsinan, the capital of Shantung province. As a matter of fact the spearheads of the expeditionary forces had already reached Tsinan when the Japanese threw in a monkey-wrench by reoccupying the whole line of the Shantung railway with a sizable force. Our Commissioner for Foreign Affairs stationed at Tsinan, Mr. Tsai Kung-shih was murdered when the Japanese occupied Tsinan. Our then Foreign Minister, General Huang Fu, was sent up to Tsinan just to find out what was happening. He failed in his mission and had to flee for his life.

I happened to be in Hsuchow where the two railway lines, the Tsingpu and Lunghai cross each other, on routine business when this disturbing news came to me. Nobody seemed to know exactly what was happening. Apparently Gen. Feng had received the news about the same time, for I got a wire from him asking me to wait for him. The next day he arrived and we hitched our private cars to the train going northward. En route we saw columns after columns of soldiers marching southward. When the train stopped at the Tai-an station we enquired for the reason of their reverse movement. We were then told by the officers that the Japanese had occupied Tsinan. To avoid a clash between the expeditionary force and the Japanese they had received orders from the Generalissimo to retreat southward. So our first effort was to find where he was. We finally located him three stations from Tai-an in an old temple where we held a momentous conference as to the appropriate course of action to be taken. One of three courses could be chosen. The first was to disregard the Japanese action and continue to march our soldiers northward through Tsinan. That would bring about immediate clash with the Japanese and might develop into a war with Japan before were ready for it. We knew sooner or later we would come to open warfare with that country, but not until we had unified our own. With a divided China, as were still then, with several "War Lords" not yet brought under our control, nothing but disaster would be the result. A second course was to stop our Northern Expedition there and then and work for the consolidation of the country from the Yellow river basin southward, leaving the northern provinces at the mercy of the "War Lords." This would have impeded the realization of our objective to unify the whole country. A third course was to move our forces westward away from Shantung and then continue our march northward through Honan into Hopei with the capture of Peking as our goal.

The conference decided to follow the third course and I was commissioned to proceed to Tsinan to negotiate with the Japanese military commander. It was a hazardous undertaking knowing what had already happened to Mr. Tsai and General Huang Fu, but having faith in the protective arms of a loving Father, I accepted it. Taking two secretaries with me we immediately commandeered a locomotive and two cars and cautiously wormed our way to Tsinan. We first telegraphed to the Tsinan station as to who were aboard the special train and to the object of our unusual visit. This message was to be conveyed to the general in command of the Japanese forces there. Whether my reputation had anything to do with it or not, we received word that we would be given safe conduct. Arriving at the Tsinan station we went to call on the General Fukuda the Japanese commander who received us without any delay. An understanding was soon reached, namely, that if our expeditionary forces should refrain from marching across the Shantung railway line, the Japanese would not impede our actions whatever. In order words they would not interfere with our internal conflict. It was very plain that by reoccupying the Shantung railways with their forces, they were already violating their neutrality. No amount of words could absolve them. I purposely refrained from raising this point in our interview, reserving that for diplomatic action later. What I wanted to accomplish then was that the Japanese would not send their forces outside of the railway zone.

We hurried back the next day to Tai-an and I made a detailed report to the Generalissimo. He spent most of the day in issuing orders to the various units of the expedition as to the routes they should take on their march northward. Gen. Feng was to take command of these forces after they crossed the Yellow river. The latter immediately entrained for his destination by the roundabout way by going south to Hsüchow, then westward to Chengchow and again northward to Honan. Finding that the Northern Expedition could again resume its march northward and in order to get some rest after the strenuous

Chapter 15   The Northern Expedition

days in meeting a difficult situation, it was suggested that we should pay a visit to the sacred mountain of Taishan only a few miles from our railway station. A party of about thirty people, besides a small bodyguard, accompanied the Generalissimo on this trip of sightseeing. Some went on horseback and others resorted to the sedan-chairs. It was fairly late in the afternoon when we got started and intended to stay at a temple at the foot of the mountain for the night before going up the mountain the next morning. We had barely finished our supper when a message was brought to the Generalissimo that his presence was urgently needed in Nanking. He did not disclose to us what the message was about but it must have been urgent enough for him to give up the trip to the top of Taishan, one of the five renowned sacred mountains of China. Most of the party went with the Generalissimo that evening to Nanking, while others like my^{me}self returned to our various destinations where we were duty bound.

The Expeditionary forces with Gen. Feng in command swept up northward after crossing the Yellow ^{R.}river. They were met with stiffer resistance from the remaining "War Lords" and much hard fighting was seen en route. However, their fate was sealed. On __?__ [sic] (1928) the object of the expedition was realized by capturing Peking, the stronghold of the Chihli clique which had been in power since 1911. The Generalissimo assumed personal command of the expedition when the victorious forces marched into in. Tsao K'un and his supporters had to flee for their lives and the government under him was formally dissolved. Our country once more had one united Central Government. However, much had yet to be done in getting all the provinces under its control and to remove that "monkey-wrench" from Shantung which the Japanese had thrown at the Northern Expedition by reoccupying the Shantung railways. I will refer to the latter question in another chapter.

The final establishment of a Central Government was a matter of great rejoicing throughout the country but not for the once all-powerful "War Lords" who had been mercilessly looting the people thereby making themselves millionaires and multi-millionaires. Some had their wealth safely deposited in the foreign banks and lived luxuriously in the foreign concessions or settlements. They were protected from arrest by the right of extraterritoriality which the Manchu regime had stupidly granted to the foreign powers. Some had entrusted their wealth to their underlings for safekeeping. Many of these underlings knew how their masters had amassed their wealth and took advantage of the situation by "looting" the masters in turn. These unfortunate "War Lords," although once had their words for law and could put any person to death at their whims, were now helpless. They would not dare to sue their underlings in courts. It was said that one of these "War Lords" Nyi Tz'e-ts'ing, former Governor of Anhui province had died a pauper. Another story was told of "War Lord" Wu Hsing-chiuan, former Governor of Heilungchiang [Heilungkiang] province who met his death when the train carrying the all-powerful Chang Tso-lin was blown up by a bomb. Wu was notorious for his ability to fleece his people and had amassed a fabulous wealth. The King of Hades on hearing of his death had arranged a magnificent dinner party in his honour. The King wanted Wu to cough up some of his ill-gotten wealth. When the dinner was about over, the King asked him how much money did he bring with him. Wu had a habit of stammering when placed in a difficult situation, so he just blurted out with one sentence: "I d-d-didn't br-br-bring even one c-c-cent with me!" I often wonder why some people should be so foolish as to make the purpose of their lives merely chasing after wealth.

To return to my story of the Northern Expedition, the overthrowing of the "War Lords" had a great sobering influence all over the country. The Governors of all the provinces pledged their support of the Central Government and obeyed its orders. Even Chang Hsueh-liang, the son of Chang Tso-lin who had inherited his father's power and wealth, also pledged his support. New Governors were appointed for the Three Eastern Provinces and they took orders from Nanking. The Young Marshall, as he was generally called by and known to the foreign nations, took in the situation graciously and was much liked by people who came in contact with him. There was no further fighting in any part of the country. All the military forces were placed under the War Ministry of the Central Government. The Ministry of Communications now exercised full authority over all the railways of the country and other public utilities. Great efforts were made to improve and extend them and much attention was given to the construction of roads. A detailed plan was worked out earmarking which were national taxes and which were provincial. But the greatest attention was given to the carrying out of the last part of Dr. Sun's will, namely, to terminate the unequal treaties with the foreign powers and I was appointed the Foreign Minister for the fourth time.

Chapter 16

Recovery of our Sovereignty Rights

When I accepted the appointment of Foreign Minister, I felt certain that I could at last bring about the termination of our unequal treaties. Hitherto I had not succeeded simply because of the instability of the central government. I had entertained high hopes of persuading the various countries to agree to a revision of our treaties on the ground of fairness and justice, although I was aware that on the one hand we had then two "central" governments and on the other privileges once obtained would be most reluctantly surrendered. However, both the "southern" government and the "northern" government had put up a united front on foreign affairs since the days of the Paris Peace Conference when we succeeded to recover our rights in Shantung after arduous and protracted negotiations with Japan. In our fight over the Shantung question the United States government had rendered to us most sympathetic assistance while the other governments also gave their support to our just cause by their tacit acceptance. Our "walking out" on the Peace Conference, when the treaty was being signed between the Allied nations and Germany at Versailles, was not considered as an act of offence to the Allied governments. We continued to take part in the deliberations of the Conference over the treaties with the other enemy states and eventually signed them jointly with the other Allied nations. I always maintain that if one has a just and right cause, eventually it will materialize, for one of the strong points of man is that he is fundamentally a believer in justice. What is needed is to convince him that you have a just cause. My apparent failure in having our unequal treaties duly revised during my former occupancy of the Foreign Office had, however, paved the way for my final success. The nations of the world were being convinced that China had a just and right cause to ask for a revision of her unequal treaties. The instability of the "northern" government was the

Chapter 16   Recovery of our Sovereignty Rights

real reason for my failure to accomplish it then.

With a united and stable central government over the whole of China, I was now in a position to hammer home the justice of our cause on the conscience of the nations concerned. One nation after another agreed to have these treaties terminated and in their place new treaties based on equality were signed. During my administration as head of the Foreign Office I had sewed up no less than 37 (?) [sic] new treaties according to China what these nations would have others accorded to them. But it required a good deal of tact in persuading them to do so. Before I describe how I succeeded in my separate negotiations with the representatives of these countries, I must turn first to my maneuvers with Japan once more over the second occupation of our Shantung railway during our Northern Expedition.

Why did the Japanese make another blunder by reoccupying the Shantung railway when they had returned it to China after the World War I has always been a puzzle to me. Should their intention be to stop our Northern Expedition, then it would have been impossible unless they should have occupied a line running from Shantung to the northwestern corner of our immense territory, as our forces could have gone north by many routes open to us. Had they intended to start a full scale war with China? If so, their military commander in Tsinan would not have agreed to keep his forces within the railway zone. The likely reason for their action was to create an "incident" in case our forces should march straight on northward over the Shantung railway. When I was asked to proceed to Tsinan to investigate personally what was happening there, I followed the last line of reasoning, so made an arrangement with General Fukuda, to wit: our Expeditionary forces would retrain from crossing the railway but would move northward to the west of Tsinan, and the Japanese forces would be contained within the railway zone. Even an "incident" was thus avoided!

After I assumed my work as the Foreign Minister in Nanking, one of the first matters I turned my attention to was to start negotiations with the then Japanese Minister to China, Mr. Yoshizawa, for the withdrawal of the Japanese forces from the Shantung railway. The Japanese really had nothing whatever to defend their case. The object of our Northern Expedition was to sweep away the War Lords from the northern provinces and to put the whole country under one central government. It was purely an internal affair. No outside nation could interfere. We had a fair and just case to demand their withdrawal from the railway zone. The negotiations went along fairly smoothly and an agreement was reached and their forces were withdrawn soon thereafter.

I would like to relate an interesting episode during the last session of our negotiations. It was held in my home in Shanghai. Mr. Yoshizawa was then residing in Shanghai. To make it convenient for both of us, several sessions of our negotiations were held there. It happened that we wanted to finish our work before my return to Nanking, so by mutual consent we had our last session in the evening after supper. We were discussing rather intently over the finishing touches on our agreement and did not realize that it was raining very hard outside. The street where my house was located was either badly drained or rather on a low level. Soon it turned into a river. To our surprise when the session was over we found a number of newspapermen waiting outside of the gate for news of the final outcome of our negotiations. They were standing ankle-deep in the running waters! To this day I have very high admiration for these news "hounds" who would never allow anything to keep them away from gathering news for their papers. Until then I did not fully realize that but for their intrepid hunt for news, the papers we read every morning would not be able to give us such an interesting and informative account of what are happening all over the world.

After the formal abolition of the Peking regime, most of the diplomatic representatives accredited to China had to move to Nanking, the capital of Nationalist China. In Peking the diplomats were concentrated in an area generally know as the Legations Quarters. Most of the Legations had substantial buildings and spacious compounds. The Legation Quarters constituted "a state within a state." It had its own police force backed up by the various garrison quartered within its walls. In times of emergency the gates leading into the Legation Quarters were closed and guarded. We saw to it that this unusual "state within a state" should not be permitted to repeat itself in Nanking. We recognized and accorded to the diplomatic representatives such special privileges as are generally allowed in other countries of the world, no less but no more. So the various legations were set up in different parts of the city.

It was my privilege as well as my duty to contact these diplomatic

Chapter 16   Recovery of our Sovereignty Rights

representatives with a view of persuading their governments to agree to the revision of the unequal treaties. I knew that I would not get the quickest results if I tackled the question by calling them together for a conference. So I followed the line of least resistance by picking out a number of them whose governments were influenced most by the support of their people and these people were more open and liberally minded. I believed then, as I still believe now, that wide publicity tactfully handled, would get the best and quickest results for any just and right cause. I therefore turned my attention first to the press. The central theme of my publicity campaign was to demonstrate that the benefits obtained through the unequal treaties by the privileged few who had established their business in China were much outweighed by the loss of trade to their nationals at home as a result of resentment from the Chinese people on a wide scale. I soon found that China had a good press in the leading countries of the world. I then began negotiations with the diplomatic representatives themselves separately and severally, also taking care that the more liberally mined were to be tackled first.

The countries that had invested quite heavily in China, either through their nationals or by the governments concerned were Great Britain, France, Russia, Belgium, the Netherlands and Germany. The United States of America had held no concessions in China. Although the Americans were among the first to trade with China, her interests were purely of commercial nature. Their investments in missionary and philanthropic work, though, were quite extensive. Either in commerce or in cultural work there were no political strings attached. But the American nationals in China also enjoyed extraterritorial rights, having the benefit of the most favoured nation clause in her treaties with China. The American Government and particularly the American people have always shown their great friendship for China as evidenced by their opposition to the partition of China, the first country to return the Boxer indemnity, and to accord recognition to the Republic of China. So I took it for granted that the United States of America would be among the first to agree to the revision of our unequal treaties. Russia and Germany were already out of the picture. The countries with whom I had to deal were narrowed down to Great Britain, France and the rest of the other nations which had treaty relations with China. But the country which I had to handle with gloved hands was Japan. She was acknowledged as one of the Great Powers only after the Russo-Japanese War. Just like any "nuvo riche" (nouveau riche) she would want to show off whenever there was an opportunity. I was fully aware of her designs upon China in particular and her conquest of the world in general. Tanaka's secret memorial to his Emperor was the blueprint of Japan's plan for world domination. I succeeded in getting a copy of it and had it translated into several languages in order to give due warning to the chancelleries of the important countries. Unfortunately it fell upon deaf ears. Not until the stealthy attack on Pearl Harbour, the sweeping conquest of the Pacific Islands, and the hammering of Japanese forces at the gates of India, when it was realized that Tanaka's Memorial was not a myth at all. So I took particular care in handling Japan. My strategy was to negotiate with Great Britain and France first and to keep Japan in a friendly mood without arousing her suspicions but to string her along with the other countries.

Among the diplomatic representatives I found in Sir Miles Lampson (now Lord Killearn), the British Minister, a man of keen intelligence, versatile and sympathetic to the aspiration of China for a full equality in the family of nations. Great Britain had been playing a leading part not only in China but in the world in general in the field of diplomacy. So I gave my full attention to winning the British Government through Sir Miles to agree to revise our unequal treaty. At the time when Sir Miles was appointed as the accredited diplomatic representative to China, there were embittered feelings in China against the British as a result of the shooting affray in the British Concession in Shanghai. I took advantage of the situation by reminding Sir Miles that we could live down these feelings by positive actions of fair play on the part of Great Britain. I pointed out to him the golden opportunity for such a positive action as presented by concluding a new treaty with China according to her full equality. Realizing the strong influence of Great Britain over the other countries, I knew that my battle for the success of terminating the much resented unequal treaties would have won, should I succeed to win her over first. So I concentrated my efforts on him and received a very sympathetic response. He was ably assisted by Mr (?) [sic] Teichmen, the Counsellor of the Legation and Mr. Merrill Hewlett, the British Consul-General stationed in Nanking. In due course, I was given

Chapter 16 Recovery of our Sovereignty Rights

assurance that the British Government was prepared to enter into a new treaty with us. Thereupon I began negotiations with the diplomatic representatives of the other countries, still following my plan of dealing with them separately and severally. As soon as I was assured by a majority of the countries which had treaty relation with us that they were ready to sign a treaty with us based on equal and reciprocal treatment, I then formally approached the Japanese Minister on this matter.

In my contact with the Japanese diplomatic officials, I found them to be men of very excellent education and generally well informed of the world situation. They were quite pleasant to deal with. Even in our headlong collision at the Paris Peace Conference over the Shantung question, both sides maintained dignity and decorum. Besides, I have quite an admiration for the Japanese people. They are industrious and thrifty. In less than a century since Commodore Perry knocked at the gates of Japan, they have brought their country out of a medieval state to a modern Power. What they lack in initiative, it is more than compensated by their ability to improve upon what they have learned from other countries. But there was a section of their people particularly a section of the military people, who conceived the erroneous idea that the Japanese Empire was destined to dominate the whole world as evidenced by General Tanaka's Memorial. In my dealings with the Japanese diplomats, I had constantly to bear in mind this handicap they were under from that quarter, usually known to the world as jingoism.

Although I have to divert from my subject under this chapter, I could not help relate an interview I had with Mr. Takahashi who was then the veteran Finance Minister in Admiral Saigo's [sic] cabinet. By the end of 1936 I was making a holiday visit to Japan and I felt that I should pay courtesy calls on the leading statesmen. In the course of our conversation through interpreters, I decried the imminent danger of a second Sino-Japanese war which would be most ruinous to both of our countries. I was expecting only a non-committal answer from him. To my surprise he gave me a most vivid and lucid statement of his view. He first pointed out to me, with full apologies for his initial statement, that in so far as military strength was concerned the Japanese could easily win the war. He then went to state three other reasons why his country could never come out victorious in a war with China. The first was the immense size of China. He made a gesture by throwing out both of his hands as if spreading a carpet. I could not guess what he was demonstrating as he was speaking in Japanese. When interpreted, he was showing that the entire Japanese military force of five million men would not be sufficient to cover the whole of China. This point was clearly vindicated after the actual war was started in 1937 and waged throughout the World War II. The Japanese did not use all their military forces in China but about two to three million men were badly bogged down only over a portion of China. They occupied important cities and strategic points in the portion they occupied but our guerillas did easily march across their lines and inflicted heavy damages to the railways and other lines of communication.

The second reason why Japan could not win a war with China was her weakness in financial and economic resources. Again he demonstrated by patting his own back, meaning to say that Japan could not add more load to her financial back. He said there were only three sources to fill the war chest. One was to increase taxation on the people. By patting his own back, he meant to say that the Japanese people could not carry any further financial burden in the form of additional taxation. A second source was to issue debentures. He told me very frankly that over 50% of the debentures issued by the Japanese Government then were being used to pay the expenses of the government. The Japanese people could take only a little over 40%. Any further issues would only tend to inflate the currency. One other way was to secure foreign loans. He pointed out that the countries that had the money to loan, meaning the United States of America and Great Britain but did not openly mention them, would not make them once there was war between Japan and China, and the countries that would like to extend loans to Japan unfortunately of course did not have the money to loan, meaning Germany and Italy, but also did not mention names.

The third reason that a war with China would only work harm for Japan, is in that his country had achieved success hitherto through the sympathy and good will of the western nations, meaning again Great Britain and America without mentioning them by name. I was rather struck by this third reason which was distinctly of a moral and spiritual nature and I believe Mr. Takahashi was not only sincere in his statement but also showed his calibre as a great statesman. Japan would certainly lose the sympathy of all freedom-loving peoples of the world by carrying on aggressive warfare against a peaceful neighbour. He had been resolutely opposing any such war against China. He was then, I believe 83 years old and yet in less than two months after this memorable interview he was assassinated, together with couple of the other cabinet ministers who had opposed war with China, by young military officers. The military jingoists soon thereafter plunged Japan into the abyss of utter defeat by attacking China first, followed by open warfare with America and Great Britain.

The reason for my narrating this interview was to show that Japan was not wanting in men of high statesmanship. Only unfortunately their sound and well-reasoned advice was not listened to by these jingoists. I am still of the opinion that Japan is bound to play a leading role in the affairs of the world, provided this jingoistic spirit should never be allowed to rear its ugly head again.

Now, I will continue my story how China regained her sovereignty rights. I knew that if I had approached Japan first on this question I would most likely butt my head against a stone wall. Ordinarily, I should have done so, since the Japanese had gone through the same experience as China had in her dealings with foreign countries. It was thought that she would be better inclined to show sympathy to China when the latter was endeavoring to recover her sovereignty rights. I did not adopt this procedure because I felt I would only arouse her suspicion that she was the first country to be asked to give up rights in China which she had only recently acquired by following the pattern of other great Powers. Her amour-propre would be much hurt. Great Britain, on the other hand, would not feel hurt if she were approached first. She had been leading in the world affairs for several centuries by this time. Moreover, the British people have a keen sense for fair play and I knew that the justice of our cause would appeal to their sense of fair play. Meanwhile I kept Japan informed of what I was working for without formally raising the question, but I knew that after the majority of the countries should agree to revise their treaties with China, Japan would follow suit.

After lining up all the countries to agree to sign a new treaty with China, I had these treaties ready for signature. I do not believe that any chancellery of the world had ever been as busy as our Foreign

Office during the days when these treaties were signed. We had to have all our stenographers pounding at their typewriters days and nights. I remember on one day I had to sign treaties with four Ministers and among them was the British Minister, Sir Miles Lampson. While waiting for his turn in the late hours of the evening for the papers to get ready, we whiled away our time by having a game of bridge. So we combined work with play, and it was work with play that did not make us dull boys!

Chapter 17

Dreams of an Industrialized China

From boyhood days it has been taught in China that the strength of a nation depends upon the prosperity of its people. This has been well borne out by the successive rise and fall of the dynasties in China and similar rise and fall of the world empires. No nation can be considered strong unless it is able to defend itself against any foreign attack. This calls for three principal factors, namely, sufficient manpower, ability to organize, and great natural resources. China, as a nation, has always maintained its ability to defend itself. It has never indulged in making any aggressive warfare throughout its long history, for it is the profound belief of our people that wars only end in bringing destruction not only to the victims but to the victors as well, unless they are for the defense of the nation. In fact China has engaged in many wars of self-defense. Thanks to its ever increasing manpower ability to organize and almost inexhaustible natural resources, it has always been able to defend itself in the end. In the two instances when China was apparently overpowered by the Mongols and the Manchus under the Yuan and Ts'ing dynasties, yet the spirit of resistance to foreign invasions never died. In the end it came out victorious. Not only it regained its full independence but as a result of centuries-old struggles it succeeded to absorb both the Mongols and the Manchus until they became part and parcel of the Chinese people.

Our contact with the seafaring powers of the west, particularly the Dutch, the British and the French, in the 18th and 19th centuries had brought about a new angle to the question of self-defense. Up to that time our defense was concerned mainly with the nomads from the north but on land. Now came potential invaders from the sea. The Dutch had invaded and once occupied our biggest island on our coast now known in the west as Formosa and the British and the French had no trouble to seize our other islands along the coast. Not only they had superior weapons, but they could also move rapidly from one end of the coast to another. Sea warfare was entirely new to China and in fact China was entirely at the mercy of these seafaring powers, so much so that China was mapped out for partition among these powers, as what actually happened to Africa, the Americas and the islands in the Pacific and other oceans. The huge size of our country, the immense number of our population and the high intelligence of our people constituted the main factors in protecting our independence. Above all is our intense love for freedom, so manifestly revealed in our literature and history. Fortunately the counsel of those of the west who had taken the trouble to study up our literature and history had prevailed upon their governments to refrain from carrying out their intention to divide up China.

It was at this juncture when our love for freedom exerted itself by overthrowing the Manchu dynasty and the establishment of the Republic. It also served as a clear warning that China would not tolerate any alien domination over her. Politically speaking, we have thus regained our independence but much has yet to be done to build up our country economically and to free ourselves from financial domination of the western powers. From time immemorial our ancestors have taught us to place a high value on moral and cultural attainments and to discourage the amassment of wealth. Some of their statements may sound to be somewhat farfetched, as for instance that "no righteous man could be rich and neither could a rich man be righteous." Yet fundamentally, it is a truism that righteousness should be sought after first. "Seek ye first the Kingdom of God and His righteousness; and all these things shall be added unto you," so said Jesus Christ. The statement I quoted above was made centuries before Jesus delivered His sermon on the Mount. The discouragement that our forefathers had placed on wealth has been, in my opinion, the deterring influence on the economic development of our people. Vast amount of latent wealth is still hidden under the immense territory of our country and greater amount of wealth could be brought into being by bringing industries to our people.

The amassing of wealth merely for personal gains and glorification is very different from creating wealth for the good of the nation as a whole. The same is true for individual nations to amass wealth for their own glorification at the expense of other nations. After the discovery of other continents throughout the whole expanse of this globe, there was a tendency among the seafaring powers to grab the wealth of the world for their own use and possession at the expense of the inhabitants already existing on these continents. Not only their gold precious stones and other articles of value were taken from them in the first processes of exploitation, even their lands were occupied, and some nations stooped so low as to capture large number of their inhabitants and sold them in the slave markets. Our forefathers had only individuals in mind when they admonished and discouraged the amassing of wealth among our own people. Their teachings had such a nationwide influence on our people so that before our contact with the western peoples there were hardly any individual Chinese who could be termed as "rich." The section of our people who were most highly respected were the scholars, most of whom had nothing more than a safe margin of mere existence. The merchants came last in the scale of respectability of the four principal sections of the people, tailing behind the scholars, the farmers and the artisans. Even these merchants took care not to amass wealth by unfair means. Hence there was a strong belief among the western peoples who came to trade with us that "a Chinaman's word is as good as his bond," meaning of course the word of a Chinese merchant.

Nowadays, a merchant is much better respected, especially a well-educated one. In the old days before the advent of western education, a scholar was only interested in classical literature and philosophy. The imperial examinations only tested the ability of the contestants for excellency [excellence] in composition and poetry. Knowledge of arts, sciences and engineering was not required at these examinations. The ratio between the number of successful contestants and that of the unsuccessful ones was so great that only a very small portion of them could attain the distinction of obtaining the degree of Hsiu-tsai, corresponding to the modern degree of Bachelor of Arts and the number became less and less as they passed their successive examinations up to the imperial examination when the degree of Han-lin, the Flowers of the Scholars was conferred on the successful candidates. However, these scholars though highly honoured for their brilliant scholarship, had in most cases very little worldly possessions. They made up what the West would call the "White-collar" class.

Now, this centuries-old system was swept away at the beginning of the present century when modern schools were being established throughout the country giving our students opportunities to acquire knowledge of other branches of learning besides literature. This ushered in a new era for our country, the beginning of an industrialized China.

An industrialized China must be based on the basis of freedom. There should be no toleration for capitalists to dominate the industries, nor should labour be allowed to overlord them. There is a third form of domination in the form of States Socialism when industries are run in the name of the State and to be owned by the State. This we must scrupulously guard against. Fortunately, there should not be and would not have much conflict between the employer and employee. The Chinese conception of the relation between the two is largely based on "family" understanding. The employer is like the head of a family while the employee or employees are treated like members of the family, each conscious of his position and responsibilities.

It might be pointed out that this family relationship could only be applied to small units such as a shop or even a small factory. But when we come to big industrial enterprises where the employer is made up of a large number of people who finance them and the employee runs into thousands and hundreds of thousands, it would be impossible for the maintenance of any family conception of their relationship. The kind of an industrial China we wish to see her developed into would be composed of large industries. Could such relationship be maintained in large industries? My answer is a positive Yes and I will state the reason for my answer.

Our people have a profound respect for a good tradition, any tradition that has proved to be beneficial to human relationship in the centuries of their existence. Human beings from the time of their birth to the time of their departure from life on earth must go through certain stages when they are either entirely helpless or when they need support and good care. In either case this help must come from people who love them and care for them, either from their parents when they are young or from their children when they are old. The first part is true all over the world and even among all living begins. If not, then life shall no longer exist. But it is on the second part that differentiates the relationship between human beings from the other living existence, namely the care of the old.

This care of the old is distinctly a human trait. Only human beings care for the aged people, but this strong human sense has taken various forms among the nations of the world. One form is founded on the system of pensions. When people reach certain age they are pensioned off. The institutions that employ them, whether government, institutional [sic] or business, set aside funds for this purpose either entirely by the employing organs or jointly by such organs and their employees. These pensions are necessarily smaller than the salaries or wages hitherto paid to them but in most cases are sufficient to meet their daily needs, naturally at reduced amounts.

Another form is in life insurance for which the insured pays a stipulated amount and a stipulated period for a life insurance policy. When that policy is fully paid up the insured gets a lump sum, if still living, or monthly installments thereby enabling him to meet his daily needs in his old age.

Then in some countries there are Homes for the Old founded by philanthropic institutions where the aged people could find their daily needs. Such Homes are naturally few in number and could not give much comfort to the old people who have no other places to go to.

These and possibly other ways have been devised to help the aged people and they have proved to be very helpful, but fundamentally all such means lack love and personal contact with their beloved ones. From time immemorial the Chinese people have been indoctrinated with the basic idea that as the young require the love and help from parents, so the children have been taught to love and look after their aged parents or near relatives as old aunts and uncles. This explains why the Chinese family is usually housed together, unlike most Western families where the parents and their young children constitute a family unit. The children as they grow up make their own homes and let their aging parents shift for themselves.

This basic idea of family relationship is extended beyond the blood ties. Employers and employees after long associations together feel toward each other like members of the same family. They generate a feeling of mutual helpfulness which is what I would like to see developed in large industrial organizations in China. I have a conviction in my belief that such will be the case as China enters into the field of large industries.

China is quite capable of developing into an industrialized nation.

She has the necessary ingredients for large industries: a large population with labourers hard working and skillful, a vast amount of raw materials and a continental size of land with long and wide rivers and with a gigantic ocean front facing the Pacific. What she lacks is the know-how of installing modern industrial machines and running them. In this she has to learn from the western nations. A start has already been made in the sending of thousands of students to western industrialized countries and in the founding of technical and industrial schools and colleges in China.

Chapter 18

Continuous Growth of China

The origin of the Chinese people is lost in the haze of ancient history where their forefathers first lived cannot be accurately traced. The first mention about this ever extending population referred to an area at the sources of the Yellow River in the present provinces of Kansu and southern Sinkiang, northwestern corner of the present day China. From there in the course of about forty centuries it spread first eastward towards the Pacific coast and then southward, crossing the Yangtze River and finally reached the basin of the Pearl River where the provinces of Kwangsi and Kwangtung are now located. This extension has been made gradually but steadily. However, there were two periods when it took on a wide spread. The first was during the Han dynasty. In the course of a single century the domain of the Chinese people reached the Pacific coast and the Yangtze River basin. Under the Tang dynasty they overran the whole south, their influence was being felt in the whole southern area of Asia. It is significant that the people in the north called themselves the Han people (漢人) and their literature as Han literature (漢文) while the people in the south styled themselves as Tang people (唐人) and their literature as Tang literature (唐文). In other words the area in which the Chinese people lived before the Tang dynasty was confined between the Yangtze River basin and the snowy north now generally known as Siberia. Beginning with the Tang dynasty it spread quite rapidly to the south of the Yangtze basin. This constant growth does not imply military conquests alone for our people never believed in the use of force to enlarge their domain.

From ancient times to the present we maintain constantly the value of virtue in winning the hearts of people. There were many Empires founded on force in the history of the world but they inevitably fell when that force spent itself. Some of them even lasted for several centuries but eventually they vanished, leaving sometimes a few vestitures of their existence because the conqueror had shown deeds of virtue besides military strength. But only virtues could endear the conquerors to the conquered, so much so that the conquered adopted the civilization of the conquerors and merged with them as one people. The conquest of England by the Normans and that of Western Europe by the Romans are another type of conquest. In such cases it is the conquerors who merged with the conquered. England has remained the home of the English and Western Europe has splitted [split] into the numerous countries in the area with different names and nationalities. Today we could find the Normans only in Normandy which is a province of France. Similarly, only the people who live in Rome, the present capital of Italy, might be termed Romans.

The expansion of China is entirely based on the exhibition of virtue, not the virtue of a single person or a number of persons but of the whole people. There are two Chinese Characters which show the marked difference between willing merger of the conquered with the conquerors and forced submission of the conquered to the conquerors. They are 霸 "Pa" and 王 "Wang." "Pa" is the doctrine of forcing someone to do your bidding while Wang is that of willing cooperation of one with another. Our philosophers and statesmen have repeatedly maintained and taught our people the importance of willing cooperation between each other. Force could only bring about temporary subjugation, while virtue touches one's heart and he becomes your friend and cooperator forever.

The Chinese character for virtue is 德 Te. Our conception of virtue exactly coincides with the Christian conception of love, which is clearly expressed by Jesus Christ Himself: "Love the Lord thy God with all thy heart, with all thy soul, with all thy mind and with all thy strength and love thy neighbour as thy self." This conception of love will in the end bring about international understanding and cooperation.

However, there are two ways of reaching the same end. One is positive while the other is negative. Love takes the positive way and is best expressed in: "Do to another as you would have another do to you." The Chinese conception of virtue is: "Do not do to another what you do not want another to do to you." Each has its advantages and disadvantages.

Chapter 18 Continuous Growth of China

The positive way gets quicker results. This explains the rapidity in the spreading of Christianity throughout the world, through schools, hospitals and other agencies wherein services of good deeds are being rendered. But it leads to conflicts and often to bloody wars, not only between Christians and non-Christians but even between the Christians themselves. When one bends on doing something to and for another, the other may resent to what you do. This would engender conflicts of opinions and if persistently followed up would even bring about bloody wars. Take for instance the so-called Holy Wars, when Christian princes followed by zealous armies against the Turks for the possession of the Holy Land, present such a typical case of positive attempts to bring Christianity to an "infidel" people. Even among the Christians themselves, bloody wars had been waged between the Catholic and Protestant sections of the various European nations. Millions had shed blood simply because one section was determined to defend the Holy Church with a Pope at the head of it, while the other section was equally determined to have no Pope at the head of their Church. Fundamentally they had no difference in their religious conceptions. The only difference was the management of the Church. The Catholics wanted the Church to be under a Pope since it was established under St. Peter as their first Pope, while the Protestants defied the authority of the Pope and would willingly lay down their lives against the Pope. These bloody conflicts lasted many years and in some of the European countries several decades.

These conflicts and wars are the results of positive actions. China has been free of any such conflicts due to religious convictions, for their philosophy of life is on the negative side. If one does not want another to impose anything on him, then he should refrain from imposing anything on others. This attitude brings about what is generally termed as tolerance. I believe that the peoples of the present world have come to learn the value of tolerance not only in religious tenets but also in political doctrines. Each person is to have freedom in any realm of his life, whether it is in his religious beliefs, political activities, industrial enterprises, or institutional organizations.

This spirit of tolerance so widespread among our people has proved to be one of the cornerstones on which the nation has thrived and expanded. From a small corner in the northwestern part of China it has spread over an area now even larger than the whole of Europe and has the largest population among the nations of the world. While Christianity will decidedly influence our people to take on a more positive attitude in the life of our people, I have not any doubt that it will never induce us to abandon the spirit of tolerance. I have been a Christian all my life. Although I was brought up in a Christian family of the Anglican Church, I associated myself freely with Christians of any of the denominational Churches of the Protestant branch of Christianity. In fact I harbour no antagonism against the Catholics either. In my younger days I had kept away from people who did not embrace Christianity in their religious beliefs. As I grew more mature in mind I came to realize that it is not the kind of religion a person believes or the form of worship he practices that accounts for his salvation. The vital and essential criterion is how he lives his life. Is it in conformity with the wishes of his Creator and in carrying out His will by being good and doing good? With this criterion in view one cannot but be tolerant towards other people and follow both principles of "Do to another what you wish another do to you" and "Do not do to another what you do not wish another do to you." I firmly believe that because of our practice of tolerance that we have been privileged to live so long for over forty centuries from the time history was written for the first time in China.

Chapter 19

Characteristics of the Chinese People

People all over the world react to a given situation more or less alike. They are happy when they get what they want and sad over their losses. They are satisfied over fair and courteous treatment but get angry if frustrated or maltreated. However, different peoples have some particular characteristics of their own. The Americans are open-minded and easy going, while the Englishmen are more formal and reserved. The Scotchmen are noted for their frugality but the Frenchmen being rather debonair spend their money more easily.

Our people have some characteristics of our own. One of them is tolerance which I have dwelt upon in a previous chapter as the cornerstone upon which the continuous growth of our country is based. This spirit of tolerance enables our people to get along well with other peoples irrespective of colour, race or religion. We have among us Taoists, Confucianists, Buddhists, Mohammedans, Christians (both Catholics and Protestants) and even Jews.

The Taoism and Confucianism have their origins in China, being led by two great teachers, Li-Er, generally and better known as Lao-Tze, and Confucius, but Buddhism, Mohammedanism and Christianity have been brought to China from foreign lands. The Jews came to China at the beginning of the Christian area. There was quite a large colony of the Jews in Honan. Their famous synagogue in Kaifong, the capital of the province, was a landmark for a long time. But the Jews have lost their identity when they were gradually being merged with our people. No one could now point out any particular place in China as the home of their descendants.

Buddhism was introduced into China from India. At one time there must have been many Indian Buddhists in our midst. Under Emperor ____ [sic] of the Tang dynasty, a delegation headed by a famous monk, now generally known as the Tang Monk, went to India for the

Holy Scripture of Buddhism, which was later translated into Chinese.

How Mohammendanism [Mohammedanism] was brought to China has remained a puzzle. It is most probable that it came with an Arabic tribe which settled down in the very corner of the country, the northwestern provinces where the original Chinese ancestors once lived. To this day there is a large section of the part of the country inhabited largely by people who embrace the religion of the true Prophet. In every other way they are Chinese, speaking the same language, eating the same kind of food and wearing the same kind of dress. Their assimilation with Chinese has been as thorough and gradual as the Jews, except that the latter have lost their identity and have not kept up their Jewish synagogues while the worshippers of Mohammed have built mosques wherever they move into and settle down. Except for their form of religious worship one is unable to differentiate them from any other Chinese who may follow other forms of worship.

Christianity came to China at a much later date. The Catholic Jesuits came couple of centuries before the advance of the Protestants pioneered by Morrison. The number of our people who believe in Christianity still constitute a small percentage of our population, although already they are running into tens of millions. It is my belief that in due course of time they are likely to reach the largest number of our ever growing population. Ever since the founding of Christianity by Jesus Christ, the work of his eleven disciples, ably augmented by the works of Saul of Tarsus later known St. Paul, has progressed continuously through the nineteen centuries and has carried His teachings to all parts of the world. More of it will be written in a later chapter.

Whatever may be the form of worship as practiced by our people all through the forty centuries as recorded in our history, the outstanding feature is our sense of tolerance among the followers of the different religions in China. Animosities and even wars have happened in other countries of the world over religious difference, our people have been able to live together as a united nation in spite of any difference in race, colour or religion.

Another significant characteristic of our people is our sense of contentment. Over eighty percent of our people live on the soil as farmers. Their standard of living is quite simple. The men rise with the sun and toil in their fields all day long and retire as the sun sets. Their

Chapter 19 Characteristics of the Chinese People

women folks do the chores at home and often assist the men in the fields, especially during the harvest season. They have very few things to amuse them. Yet feel quite happy and content.

It is sometimes argued that contentment tends to kill ambition so the contented person seldom rises above the condition in which he finds himself after his birth. This argument is sound in so far as certain individuals are concerned who may have the marital and physical capacity to improve themselves but have no ambition to do so. The bulk of the farmers, however, have only one ambition in their lives and that is to get a good harvest from their soil. Our system of examinations did offer opportunities to those who wish to become scholars and even gain government posts if and when they showed special capacity in their scholarly achievement. The modern educational facilities will undoubtedly divert the offsprings of the farmers toward other lines of work. Whatever that may be the vital thing is to feel happy in the work they are engaged in. I believe our people are endowed with this happy contentment to a very large degree.

Family life is another characteristic of our people. The Chinese conception of a family is fundamentally much wider than that of the West. It is made up not only of the parents with their young children, as is usually understood in the West, but also of the grandparents and sometimes the great-grandparents. Oftentimes widowed aunts and orphaned nephews and nieces are included in a family. It is their strong devotion to and love for their family life that account for this spectacular aspect of a Chinese family. It amounts almost to family worship.

It is a common practice in most of the Chinese families to erect an Ancestrial Hall where the tables on each of which the names of their ancestors are written, or engraved upon. At stated intervals their descendents will appear before them and express their love for them by burning incense and offering food and fruits. They will also go and visit their ancestors' graves once a year on the day of Ts'ing Ming, a festival day signifying Clear and Bright, which falls approximately towards the end of March and the beginning of April according to the solar calendar. This is practiced throughout China. But in South China, particularly in Canton, they also visit their ancestors' graves on the Double Nine, that is the 9th day of the 9th moon, around the end of September and the beginning of October in the

149

solar calendar.

These practices tend to show that our conception of family life includes those who have departed from their lives on earth. It leads inevitably to our worship of Heaven, the Creator of Life, so similar to the Christian conception of God, the Creator of the heaven and earth and all things therein including human beings.

Capacity for hard work constitutes another characteristic of our people. Diligence in one's work that is congenial to him is universally applauded, but to be able to work hard in any form of drudgery calls for a greater applause. It is only through generations of hard working that this habit has been formed in our people. Credit must be given to our farmer ancestors who for hundreds of generations have found it worthwhile to work hard in order to get good results from their toils on the farms. This trait has been a mighty asset to our people. It is best demonstrated by our overseas Chinese when they are given greater opportunities for work with higher remunerations. That is why they become prosperous communities wherever they might migrate to.

I have personally visited many such an overseas Chinese community [sic] and felt proud of and for these fellow countrymen, in the Philippines, Singapore and Malaya, in the South Sea Islands, in Burma, Thailand and India and in the United States of America. The first immigrants were usually from what are generally known as coolies, that is, just plain workmen with hardly any education. Now their children and children's children are engaged in business, many of whom have received high education and many of them have amassed wealth of some degree and some have even become millionaires.

With the advancement of modern industries and scientific knowledge, even greater opportunities are now open to our people. Because of the habit of hard working they cannot but succeed in whatever work they happened to be engaged in.

Finally I must point out another characteristic of my people. That is their inherent intelligence. It has repeatedly been demonstrated that one could pick up any Chinese child on the street who reveals a high degree of what is now known as I. Q. when given an opportunity to learn, either in book knowledge, or in trade or business and now even in scientific research.

Chapter 19 Characteristics of the Chinese People

The recent award of a joint Nobel prize to two comparatively very young professors of physics is an example of high intelligence. These two professors were still around thirty years of age when their research work was given acknowledgment by the Noble award.

The intelligence of the Chinese people had been largely channeled into literature in the past. Science has only been given a place in the Chinese educational system in recent years, but our inherent intelligence is capable of grappling with science. In Professors Li and Yang to whom the Nobel award was recently given we have an excellent proof of this intelligence.

With these fine characteristics of our people, I feel sure that we will be able to contribute our share in the advancement of international understanding, good will and world peace among the nations of the world.

Chapter 20

A Woman's Place in China

I have often puzzled over the question of a woman's place in the life of our people. On the surface her life in China does not differ much as compared with the women of other lands. She is the life companion of her husband and the mother of their children. But her status in the family undergoes quite fundamental changes in the different stages in her life. These stages often present great differences not only in her relation to other members of the family but also when compared with the life of women in other countries.

The first stage of a woman's life in China begins after her marriage. She becomes as a sort of an adopted member of another family and begins to bear the latter's surname over her own family surname and name. Let us take the case of a girl born in the Wang family and she is called Kwei-Ying. After her marriage to a man bearing the surname of Chang she is thereafter known as Chang Wang Kwei-Ying. In the old days a girl's name is only known to her own family. No other person is to know it. We have developed a system to designate which of the Wang girls we are referring to. If she is the only daughter of the family, she will be simply called Miss Wang. In case there are several daughters in the family, each will then be called by the order of their birth, Miss Wang the eldest, or Miss Wang the second and so on. This is quite different from the title of Queen Elizabeth the Second of England. It happened there was a queen in England who was called Elizabeth and she reigned in England several centuries ago. The present reigning queen of England also bears the same name of Elizabeth so is known as Elizabeth the Second. In China any second daughter in a family has the privilege of bearing the title of the "Second" after her surname.

This stage in her life calls for submission or obedience, not so much to her hundred but to his family. There is a reigning queen in that family, her mother-in-law. When I first attended a Western University in America, I was surprised by a college "stunt" known as "hazing" when Freshmen, newly admitted to a college, were "taught" by their upper classmen — the sophomores — to behave themselves. I would not say that mothers-in-law in China actually browbeat their "newly admitted" daughters-in-law into submission but the relative position is more or less the same as that of the sophomores to the Freshmen.

A wise daughter-in-law will therefore take care not to do or say anything that may be disapproved by her mother-in-law in the affairs of their family. Her position is not dissimilar from that of a diplomat accredited to another government wherein she has to exercise much decorum and care. Otherwise she might be considered as persona non-grata, causing not only frictions in her "adopted" family but often leading to antagonism between the allied families, sometimes even to open warfare.

This stage in a woman's life is rather a trying period, particularly when the husband's family has still a number of unmarried daughters living under the same roof. It is further complicated after the arrival of her own children when extra servants have to be employed to look after them. This might be the principal reason why many young married couples prefer to live by themselves. Only family ties in China are too strongly entrenched to facilitate such schisms in it. Fortunately, the sons nowadays do not necessarily follow the same kind of work as their fathers and often find their callings in different parts of the country and may even in some foreign country. It is only natural that they live elsewhere and set up a household for themselves.

The second stage of a woman's life arrives when her children are fully grown and married. Her daughters are married off to other families but her sons will bring their wives to the home. She becomes now the "sophomore" in the "School of Family Life" and has to deal with the newly admitted "Freshmen," her daughters-in-law. The shoe now is on the other foot. She has gone through the life of a "Freshman" and has acquired knowledge in handling the situation equally tactfully. A wise mother-in-law will endear herself to them. With wide and varied experience in life she becomes their adviser in guiding them to attain full efficiency in the management of home affairs. She will be a very happy mother-in-law if and when her daughters-in-law cherish toward her the same kind of respect and love for her as for their own mothers.

This is the time of life when she enjoys most. She is still in good health and has no more family burdens to bear. Her daughters-in-law while respectful of her and doing their best to make her life happy, are likely to be occupied of their own chores. She has time now to entertain other mothers-in-law or go to their entertainments. Most often she becomes a playmate to their grandchildren, telling them bedtime stories or sing [singing] them to sleep.

This is also the time of life when she gets the highest respects from society, particularly if any of her sons has made good in life, becoming a celebrated government official or a wealthy and substantial business tycoon. She will be conferred with the distinguished title of (賢妻良母) Hsien-Chi Liang-Mu, which means the Virtuous Wife and the Munificent Mother, by public acclamation.

The final stage in a woman's life in China comes when she becomes the great grandmother of the family. She is of course in a most happy state when she is surrounded by three generations of her children, especially if and when some of them have gained prominence in the social scale of life. She is most likely well advanced in age, so is not in a physical condition to enjoy life as much as when compared with her own life at the second stage.

I must digress here to give a picture of the man's life in China. He naturally shares all the joys and happiness of a family life and in most cases it is he who beings honour and joy to the family. As a husband he brings these to his wife and when he achieves success in life, his parents get a full reflection of such success.

There is a very interesting anecdote in connection with this reflection of honour in the family. A certain well-known man who was once a Prime Minister at the Court was one day riding in his distinguished sedan chair by the bank of a river. He was then well advanced in years. Perceiving a yellow umbrella by the bank, indicating there was another person of high rank under that umbrella, he ordered his chair bearers to stop and left his sedan chair and set out on foot to meet that distinguish person. It turned out that the man under the umbrella, quietly casting his line for fishing, was no other person but his own son. The old man became very angry and began to upbraid him for impersonating a man of rank by that yellow umbrel-

Chapter 20   A Woman's Place in China

la. His son was already approaching a cycle of man's life, namely 60 years, but had never had any success in life except that he was blessed with a son who was then holding the post of the Prime Minister at the imperial court. He got up and stood respectfully before his father and said quietly: "Father, am I not entitled to enjoy the priviledge[^privilege] of life by having a father who was once a Prime Minister, and a son who is now the Prime Minister?" On reflection the anger of the old man immediately evaporated and left his son to continue fishing by the bank of the river. This story, I think, gives a precise interpretation of what is meant by a reflection of honour in a Chinese family.

A woman in China has the same vicissitude of life as any other woman in the world. She might be left a widow still in the prime of her life either with children or without. In either case she is doomed to a life of solitude, particularly when she has no issue of her own. Traditions discouraged remarriage, although there in no written law against it. The Chinese family life, however, assuages somewhat her sadness by her position in the family. She continues to be a respected member of the family, receiving the same care and affection as if her husband were still alive. But I believe it would be much better that she is not so bound by tradition which in my opinion, is not giving equal rights to the two sexes. When a man is left a widower society does not frown upon him if he gets married again. Why then should a widow be condemned to a life of solitude when her husband dies? Care and love from the family do not entirely satisfy the needs of a woman. The Western attitude towards remarriage of women is therefore more sensible. This attitude is however generally accepted also by modern China.

Chapter 21

Chinese Conception of Religion

In a previous chapter when I discussed how tolerant our people are, I mentioned the fact that the five principle religions of the world coexist in China without much friction. As a matter of fact I have known of families whose members embrace different religious beliefs and live happily together.

The father is a Confucian scholar who worships Heaven as his God, delving into documents and books which deal with Tao (道) conveying the same significance as what was stated by St. John at the very onset of his gospel: "In the beginning was the Word, and the Word was with God and the Word was God." To a Chinese scholar Tao represents the very Word of Heaven. It is invisible to the human eyes, conveys no sound to his ears, and does not reach any of his other senses but he knows it is in existence, for he is endowed with mental and spiritual powers besides his physical senses.

In the physical world one is limited by time and space. We could touch a thing when it is only near at hand. Once out of our reach we have no way to find out whether it is soft or hard, rough or smooth, hot or cold, et cetera. The same is true with sight and sound. The naked eyes could see things at a limited distance and the human ears could catch sound in a limited way. The development of modern science however, has enable us to see things at a much longer space or hear sound from much longer distances but still they are limited by the degree of power of the modern instruments bringing the objects to our eyes or the wave length of sound to our ears.

When we come to make use of our mind we break through at once both space and time. We could form mental pictures of things that are beyond the reach of our senses. Memory helps us to recall events and occasions which happened years or ages ago and our imaginations could lead us to project into the future for ages to come. Much of

Chapter 21 Chinese Conception of Religion

human progress is made through this mental process. All discoveries and inventions are the result of our mental efforts without which we would have remained in the same stage as all animals have been since creation. Some of these animals have shown skill high enough to challenge mankind. For instance, the work of the bees in building their hives, making use of or the lightest material yet with great strength and artistic task, is often a challenge to the best human architect in building a house in the same way. The only difference lies in the fact that the beehive built thousands of years ago remains the same as that of the 20th century. The bee, although exhibiting great architectural skill, does its work by instinct while a human being uses his mental power to improve his architectural ability from generation to generation.

The thatched huts of our ancestors could have no comparison whatsoever with our modern gigantic constructions. Not only that the buildings are continuously getting bigger and taller but the forms and decorations, both interior and exterior, are being improved upon in one way or another, although some of his work in certain periods of the human history is still considered superior as compared with the present century. Political considerations, economic prosperity and particularly religious enthusiasm have jointly contributed to the building of the great cathedrals which still stand today as some of the great wonders of the world.

Just as the human mental power has achieved much superior benefits to mankind as compared with his physical ability, so does his spiritual endowment surpass his mental power. Through the use of his mental power he has distinctly improved his well-being in every way. He is able to live in a better house with more cheerful surroundings and with all facilities to give him health and comfort. His house is furnished with fresh air, light and water and the disposal of waste through sewage and other means. Good roads, motorcars and steamships enable him to travel comfortably and quickly from one place to another. The present century has produced man-made wings to fly in the air and reach his designated spot on earth in as few hours as land and sea transportations used to take them in so many days or weeks to accomplish. Radio and television nowadays will bring him music and scenes to which he was denied before these wonderful inventions were made. In a thousand other ways he has more comfort than his forefathers even of the last century.

But is the modern man happier in his spiritual life? This constitutes a great enigma in a man's life. Besides his physical ability as evidenced by his five senses and his mental power as reflected in the discoveries and inventions, he is further endowed with a spiritual force which far surpasses the other two. This spiritual force leads him to a far higher plane of life. The other two planes are mundane and temporary. They last only as long as his life on earth lasts. The physical plane is hemmed in by time and space and the mental plane, although quite free from time and space and is capable of reaching out in all directions and at all times, yet it is unable to function when his life is terminated. But the spiritual plane reaches out to eternity irrespective of time and space and whether he is alive or after his death. All religions lead and guide a man to his Creator who was, is and ever shall be.

The great founders and teachers of these religions may call the Creator by a different name, whether it is Tao, Heaven, Sakyamuni, Allah or God but they mean the same Creator. Their teachings show the way to Him. It is only through this spiritual plane of man that he is led and guided to Him.

From the beginning of human existence he is conscious of this spiritual power. Long before there is any means to record and describe the working of this power, it has been passed on from generation to generation by the word of the mouth and by action and example. In China this spiritual consciousness is first shown in the worship of the departed spirits of the family. Our people have a strong conviction that the spirits of their loved ones do not die but will live forever, if during their short span of life on earth they are brought into touch with this spiritual power which calls for upright living and acts of good will for his fellow men. Gradually, by the aid of a written language the worship of this spiritual force takes on a more definite form. This force is conveyed to our people by the Chinese character of Tao (道) which the founder of Taoism, Li-Erh, better known as Lao-Tze (老子) the Old Teacher, describes so succinctly in his Bible of the Tao, Tao-Teh-Ching (道德経). It has turned out to be the shortest among the bibles of the world, leading and guiding mankind towards his Creator. It is recorded in history that Confucius once called on the Old Teacher for enlightenment upon this vital question.

Chapter 21 Chinese Conception of Religion

These two great teachers were contemporaries, only the Old Teacher was already in a very advanced age while Confucius was still a young man then.

The teaching of Taoism has been considered by some people as mere philosophy but it deals with the philosophy of life, particularly with life leading to the eternal life of the spirit. In essence it is certainly a form of religion. It urges people to be good and to do good. There are millions of people in China who follow it. The only criticism that has some solid foundation is that it is rather a passive and not an active religion. The eternal truth about life to come is fundamentally stated but couched in such deep philosophical statements that are not easily understood by the ordinary people. Great scholars have pondered over those statements and have delved into them and compared them with the facts of the kind of life the people practicing them have to follow before coming to understand what is meant by them.

The teaching of Confucius takes on a clearer objective than Tao. He uses Heaven as the name of the great Creator. It is not of course the blue sky which we can see with our human eyes but only to be conceived in our spiritual eyes. The heaven as seen by the human eyes is large and wide enough to challenge even the modern scientists. With our modern inventions we are unable to direct our eyes to soar way up into the sky and to marvel at the innumerable number of stars and planets, circling around their individual suns as our Earth goes around our Sun with the other planets encircling it together with ours.

This Heaven as conceived in our spiritual eyes represents the great and mighty powers of the Creator. We are told that Heaven is most benevolent towards the human beings on earth. He warms them with the rays of the sun and showers rains on them to give them water to drink. Sun and rains together give them sustenance in the things that are made to grow on the soil of the earth, irrespective whether we lead an upright life or are sinners against His will. However, we are cautioned about the way we live. In the solemn passages in the writings of Confucius or later further elaborated by his students, we are reminded that Heaven has eyes to see what we do, has ears to hear what we say, and keeps a detailed record of our deeds of good work or acts of sin. We are further reminded that for our deeds of good work and upright living we are to be duly rewarded but punishments shall be meted out to the sinners.

The teachings of Confucius reach a much wider circle among our people. Naturally the scholars get the first impulse of his teachings. A little boy at the beginning of his education is told in his text book that man is good by nature but gradually deteriorates as, in his growing years, he begins to err as he follows bad examples and evil influences. He is duly encouraged to be good and to do good and to avoid acts of evil. As he grows up he learns a great deal more about Heaven. In the end he becomes a firm believer in Heaven. As a scholar is on the top ladder of the social scale of our people, followed by the farmer, the artisan and the merchant, he exercises a very great influence over them. He is looked up to for guidance and leadership in social, educational and political activities of the nation. The concept of Heaven as the Supreme Being becomes so wide spread in due course of time, that in the imperial days in China, the Emperor, as the representative of his nation, would worship Heaven once a year, on the first day of the year at the Altar of Heaven in the Capital.

The other three religions have been introduced into China from abroad at different periods in her history and under different circumstances — Buddhism was in the lead. It must have been brought to China by Indian Buddhist monks. It thrived most in the Tang dynasty when Chinese monks were sent to India to study Buddhist teachings. The mission came back after many years of travel and sojourn in the land where Buddhism had its first followers. Today Buddhism has even a larger following than the Taoists or Confucianists. These are usually found among the educated and intellectuals but the bulk of our uneducated people have accepted Buddhism, for its form of worship is more realistic. Buddhistic temples could be found all over the country, even in the very interior places and high top mountains. Some of these have been beautifully constructed and in most cases give the visitors a sense of awe and respect.

How Mohammedanism was brought into China has been and is still a puzzle. In all probability it came with Arab tribes who settled down in the northwestern provinces but later penetrated into many other provinces bringing their religion with them. In the course of centuries their long residence in China has changed their nomadic habits and amalgamated with the Chinese people, retaining however

Chapter 21 Chinese Conception of Religion

their religion acclaiming Allah as the Creator with Mosques as their places of worship wherever they happen to settle down.

The story of the introduction of Christianity into China, is well-known. It is the result of concerted action by the followers of Jesus Christ in Christian countries all over the world, led first by the French Catholics, followed by the English Protestants and strengthened by missionary societies throughout the whole Christendom. After the founding of the United States of America as an independent nation in the latter part of the eighteenth century, the virile nature of the American people has demonstrated its vigour also in the field of religious propaganda in China. Although they were almost the last to enter into this field, they soon outstripped all the missionary societies from other Christian countries. Towards the end of last century and the beginning of the present century most of the Christian schools and hospitals in China have been in the hands of American missionaries. Since the advent of the communistic regime in 1948, most of them have to be withdrawn from the field, but their work will be carried on by the native workers whom they have trained and put in responsible positions. More will be said on this matter in a later chapter which deals on the struggle between freedom and communism.

Our concept of religion is based on the essence and not on the forms of worship. The essence is to know the way of the Creator through our spiritual insight and to follow His way as revealed to us in spirit. All religious teachers show to us that the Creator is a spirit and we are to love and honour Him in spirit. This broad concept enables our people to live happily together although the followers of the different religions may practice various ways of worshipping the Supreme Being. In a Chinese family nowadays, the father, the mother and the children may embrace different religions and each worships in his or her ways. The father may be a Taoist or Confucianist, the mother a Buddhist and some of the children may be Christians of many different denominations, yet they are able to dwell in the same house without any sense of antagonism between them.

The father may be sitting quietly at his desk either delving into the works of great scholars of the past generations on the subject of Tao or Heaven or meditating on the philosophy of life as seen through his spiritual eyes. The mother having embraced Buddhism may be burning incense at her altar and repeating the Buddhist rituals. The children may be reading their Christian Bible and saying their morning prayers. Each in his or her way finds satisfaction in response to the spiritual urge of the heart towards the Supreme Being. Freedom of religion has been an outstanding feature in China for so long that the introduction of other religions to China in one way or another has not brought any serious religious conflicts among our people, as some of the other nations have experienced in the centuries preceding the enunciation of that great principle of Freedom of Religion.

This great principle first found articulate expression among the settlers in the New World. These had come from countries in Europe where religious conflicts had taken the lives of many millions. To escape from religious persecutions in their native countries they ventured forth to find a place where they could worship the Supreme Being, without molestation each in his own way. So the Fathers of the American Revolution in writing a Constitution for their newly formed Republic, the United States of America had stated at the outset their insistence on the Freedom of Religion. This freedom is now incorporated in the Charter of the United Nations. Although our people have never put this principle in writing but have always upheld it in practice.

This widespread belief in religious freedom has recently taken another important turn which aims in bringing together coordinated activities between the followers of the five principal religions. It took the form of an organization called the World Red Swastika Society.

I must digress here to point out the difference between the sign of the Chinese Red Swastika from the dark swastika of the Nazis under Hitler. The character of the Chinese Swastika is written thus 卍 and is painted red while the Nazi swastika is dark and is a reverse of it. Moreover the Chinese swastika is upright and straight as compared with the Nazi swastika which is set at an angle diagonally thus 卐. It is unnecessary for me to make any comment on the dark designs of the Nazi under Hitler. There would never have been another world war but for the evil machinations of Hitler in conjunction with Mussolini in their efforts to destroy the freedom of the world. The inborn love for freedom of mankind throughout the world would not permit its destruction and at a mighty sacrifice in life and blood, these evil doers were finally crushed and uprooted.

The Chinese word of swastika means Ten Thousand. It has been in

Chapter 21 Chinese Conception of Religion

the Chinese language from the very beginning of writing as our way of accounting ends at ten thousand while in the West it ends at thousand. Instead of saying a hundred thousand we say ten ten thousand. This has always been a source of error in interpreting figures in Western language into ours and vice versa. It represents the highest in the scale of things. In the imperial days the Emperor was often referred to as the "Ten Thousand Years" while the Crown Prince as the "Thousand Years," although very few ordinary human beings live up to a hundred years. "Ten Thousand" for the Emperor and "Thousand" for the Crown Prince simply convey a mark of respect for them. The Buddhist priests have often pained a large 卍 on the breasts of sainted monks to show the same mark of respect.

The World Red Swastika Society was first organized in the Ping district of the Province of Shantung (山東濱縣) where four close friends, one a regiment commander, another the District Magistrate and their two secretaries, were often together in 1916 and 1917 discussing and praying for a spiritual inspiration for their own religious awakening. One evening during their seance they received a distinct call to start an organization which is to bring about active cooperation among the followers of all the five religions, not only in their own country but to include all the nations of the world. It is to be known as the World Red Swastika Society and to use the Red Swastika as the symbol of the Society.

When this was disclosed to their numerous friends it immediately received a hearty response. In 1918 the centre of activity was moved to Tsinan (濟南), the capital of the Province of Shantung when thirty-six men, among whom was General Tien Chung-yu (田中玉) the then Governor of Shantung, were appointed to lead the organization. From this time on it made great strides, internally by the promulgation of the Articles of Association to guide and govern its activities, and externally by spreading its work to other parts of China and to other countries. Tientsin (天津), Peking (北京) and Tsining (濟寧) were the first three cities in which the Movement took a firm root and from which it spread rapidly to other cities in the various provinces to the north, west and south of Shantung. By the end of 1928 there were over two hundred branches in nineteen provinces in China and one branch in Kobe, Japan. Since then the growth of the Movement has been phenomenal. Before the war broke out between China and Japan in 1937 the number of branches rose to nearly five hundred in China alone. Many branches were formed in Japan, one in Hong Kong and another in Singapore.

1922 should be the year marked down as the official beginning of the Movement when the Articles of Association were duly registered with and approved by the National Government of China, and Tsinan Branch was declared as the Mother Temple. On the Spring Day (立春) of that year a solemn religious ceremony was performed in the Tsinan Temple to celebrate the founding of the organization. The Spring Day, which falls every year around February 4th, has always been an important day in China. It marks the return of life when trees begin to open their new buds and all living beings have an urge to multiply themselves.

Inasmuch as the object of the Red Swastika Society is to bring about coordinated activities between the religious followers throughout the whole world, it therefore welcomes all nationalities into its membership irrespective of race, colour or creed. It aims to foster universal brotherhood and world peace by urging people to sink their differences in the tenets of their religious beliefs, their manners and customs, their languages and culture, and their colour and race.

The present century has certainly ushered in a new spirit in world cooperation. Politically, it led to the organization of the League of Nations after the First World War. Imperfect as this organization proved to be and its life was cut short by World War II, nevertheless the nations of the world absolutely refused to be discouraged by its failure. In consequence another world organization soon took shape in the founding of the United Nations right after the ending of that World War. But the world situation took another turn and might lead to a third World War. Whatever be the fate in store for it, it is quite certain that the spirit of world cooperation shall continue to grow even stronger as the years go by.

Sociably, new forces have been brought into play in many forms to foster international understanding and world peace. I will only mention a few of these forces. The Rotary Movement is one of them, started by only four men in Chicago at the beginning of the century, it now encircles the earth with nearly 5000 Rotary Clubs (1960) in over one hundred countries or areas and has in its membership of almost half-a-million of the leaders of profession and businessmen throughout the world. The Young Men's Christian Associations and the Young Women's Christian Associations, the Boy Scouts and Girl's Guides are among many other organizations which aim at world cooperation, irrespective of race, colour or creed.

The most significant is the tendency of religious bodies to work for world cooperation. Not only the different denominations of the Christian religion are showing greater toleration towards each other, but they even evince more willingness to cooperate with the followers of other religions. This has been the practice of our people. We have among us the followers of all religions and have always maintained the spirit of toleration. Now with the advent of the Red Swastika Society we wish to go beyond this spirit and seek active cooperation between them.

Chapter 22

Strong Love for Freedom

To a casual observer of our people there has always been the impression that we are rather docile and ready to comply with the wishes of others. This may be due to our spirit of tolerance and forbearance. We do not flare up easily and go into heated arguments over matters with which we are not familiar and we may seem to be giving in too readily. As a matter of fact, silence does not mean consent. We are only weighing these matters to find out their true aspects and their effects on the welfare of the people individually as well as collectively. It often takes a long period of time before we see the true state of affairs. But once they are found to be harmful to our people a strong opposition will inevitably be the result. This opposition may take different forms in its expression. Village elders may discuss them as they meet casually in their daily contacts, thereby form a public opinion on them, first in the villages and then spread to the districts and provinces and finally to the whole country. Sometimes, some individual persons after careful studies on them form a definite opinion and organize themselves into a definite and strong opposition. At first this work is being done underground but as it gathers strength it comes out in the open and does not hesitate to take up arms for their defense. Again, a strong force of opposition may emerge among those in power, thereby forcing a sharp issue between the supporters and objectors of the question. Whether the supporters or the objectors are right has to be finally decided by the nation at large. Whatever may be the form of opposition, the inevitable result is that victory always comes to the lovers of freedom as opposed to the totalitarian methods of government. Our history for over forty centuries is a constant reminder of the strong love of our people for freedom.

This love for freedom has been the main source of the strength of our people. It explains why we have been able to maintain ourselves

Chapter 22 Strong Love for Freedom

in face of internal and external enemies of freedom all these centuries with a growing population extending beyond the boundaries of our country. Indeed we feel proud that we have the largest population in any country in the world and have the longest history. Ancient Empires like the Babylonian, the Greco and the Roman Empires are now only known in history. Even more modern Empires, like those under Charlemagne, under Genghis Khan, under Napoleon could be traced only in history books. They are no longer in existence. But China under seventeen dynasties, counting only the major ones, and now under a Republican form of government, though temporarily divided at the moment when this is being written is still existing as one nation. More shall be said in a subsequent chapter on the future of our country.

The change of a dynasty in China only marks the rise and fall of a ruling family. Only twice in our long history we had a foreign prince sitting for a considerable period of time on the throne, the Yuan dynasty under the Mongols for nearly a century and the Ts'ing dynasty under the Manchus lasted for over two and a half centuries. In each case the love for freedom of our people exerted itself, not only succeeding in toppling these foreign rulers but also in our absorption of them and their cohorts with our people in a less or greater degree. A part of the Mongolian population is still in existence and they constitute the so-called Outer Mongolia. The Manchus, however, have been completely absorbed. Even in the Northeastern provinces which were once the home of the Manchus, the population there is preponderantly Chinese. The name of Manchuria is sometimes applied to these provinces but is distinctly a misnomer, for this so-called Manchuria has only a few handful [sic] of Manchu families living therein.

Dynasties may come and dynasties may go, the core of our people remains the same, with the same strong love for their land, strong love for their institutions and strong love for freedom. In the long history of our country we had to face squarely at the attempts of the enemies of freedom both internal and external.

Of the internal enemies of freedom the greatest was our Strong Man, the ruler of one of the numerous vassal states at the close of the Chow dynasty. As the ruler of his state, known at that time as Chin (秦) and situated at the northwestern corner of the country, he showed great ability as an administrator exercising his power with skill and ruthlessness. In course of time there were only seven powerful states left. The rest had been gobbled up by them. Before long, only three of them were able to maintain their independence of which the state of Chin was steadily growing more and more powerful. The state of Chi (齋) comprising then the territory from the Pacific Ocean in the East across the Yellow River in the South, reaching the Yangtze River basin and adjoining the territories of Chin and Ch'u (楚) in the West. The latter was the third of the then triumvirate states ruling over the central and western provinces of the present day China. In size Chi and Ch'u were each much larger than Chin but in strength, both militarily and politically, Chin was much superior. A struggle for supremacy was unavoidable. At one time the Strong Man of Chin was considering which of the other two he should align with to overcome the third. By dexterous maneuver of his forces, he soon defeated the stronger of the two and having accomplished that he brought the third to utter subjugation. He became then the supreme head of the nation and founded the great Chin dynasty and styled himself as the First Chin Emperor in the hope that his dynasty would live longer than even the Chow dynasty, unrealizing that any dynasty founded on power alone would not last long and the Chin dynasty ironically proved to be the shortest of them all.

Our people were at first much dazzled by his unusually skillful handling of his forces, coupled with great dexterity in statesmanship. But he committed the greatest mistake in his life by forgetting that the Chinese people would not tolerate despotism. Soon our love for freedom exerted itself. Strong criticisms arose all over the country, so much so as to enrage the Strong Man into taking vigorous steps for their suppression. The most spectacular was staged by inviting three thousand of his critics, mostly scholars of renown, to a state banquet at his court. When his distinguished guests were all decorously seated and began to partake their grand state meal, by a given signal soldiers rushed into the dining hall and hauled them off bodily to a large pit outside the capital secretly and carefully prepared for them. They were all buried alive. He thought that would end any further criticism once for all! But the opposite was the result.

Instead of more verbal opposition movements soon began to be noticed throughout the country to meet despotism by force. It came to

Chapter 22   Strong Love for Freedom

his imperial ears that his mighty military brigades were infested. In order to have these forces engaged in some military occupation away from the country, he let out a false alarm that the country was in a great danger of an invasion by the northern nomadic tribes known as the Hu's by inventing a cry throughout the country that it would be destroyed by the Hu's! He called together his courtiers and military leaders for a conference as to the best means of overcoming this eminent danger. A resolution was adopted to erect a great stone wall from the Pacific Ocean at a point now known as Shan Hai Kwan (山海關) the Gate of Mountain and Ocean, across the whole northern boundary of the country to the Mountains in the West, a distance of approximately a thousand miles. Although stones were available at the eastern end of the wall, there was a long stretch of land consisted mainly of sand dunes. The pyramids in Egypt stand today as one of the wonders of the world because of the difficulty in transporting stones from far away to where they were built. But the Great Wall is a greater wonder. It took over thirty years of hard labour to build that Wall even with practically the whole force of his soldiers consisted mainly of young men in the prime of life. By the time an order to stop the work was given they were already near fifty years old. Their officers being much older at the beginning had been replaced by younger men during the construction. But the Great Wall was still several hundred miles short of the original plan. The work had to be stopped unquestionably due to lack of available man power. The real reason for its stoppage was the fact that the aging monarch was no longer in fear of a revolt of his people backed up by his powerful cohorts. Soon thereafter, the old despot himself had to depart from this world due to old age. His son, the heir-apparent, had already gone before him so the throne was taken up by his grandson. Lacking both ability and prestige, this Second Emperor became also the last of the dynasty. The Strong Man who founded the Chin dynasty had made plans for it to last for "ten thousand" years and had styled himself as Emperor the First, was in fact the founder of the shortest dynasty in our country!

This vividly brings out the fact that the love for freedom is so strong that no despot could rule over China. Many such an attempt [sic] had been made in our long history but in every case it ended in failure, because our people would never tolerate any despotic rule.

The struggle for freedom calls for a strong love for it, coupled with an equally strong determination to achieve it. Twice in our history the country was overrun by powerful neighbours. The Mongols were the first to conquer us and they founded the Yuan dynasty which lasted nearly a century. For three generations our people struggled to regain our freedom. Millions had to migrate from the north to South China. They must have fled into all parts of the southern provinces but some had actually reached this far distant corner of the country, now known as Hong Kong. But the struggle for freedom was never given up until the Mongols were finally ousted from China under the leadership of Chu Hung-wu the founder of the Ming dynasty.

For a second time China lost her independence when the Manchus came across the Great Wall at Shan Hai Kwan. What was once a fabricated tale in the reign of the Strong Man, the First Emperor of the Chin dynasty for a private reason of his own, materialized into an actual fact nearly twenty centuries later. The year 1644 marked the beginning of another dynasty with a Manchu prince on the imperial throne. It is known as the Ts'ing dynasty, not to be confused with the Chin dynasty, but the Manchus are one of the tribes of the Nomadic Hu's against whom the Great Wall was supposed to be built for. What an irony in fate!

This foreign dynasty lasted for over two and half centuries. Our people did not regain our freedom until 1911 when the last Manchu Emperor was forced to abdicate by the leaders of the successful Revolution, so ably led by Dr. Sun Yat-sen. There is no necessity to give an account of this Revolution. Many of these leaders are still living of whom this writer is one. It is, however, quite interesting to delve into the reasons why this dynasty, so much hated by the lovers of freedom among our people, should succeed to last so long.

The first Manchu Emperor was a man possessing great versatility of mind. He knew his military strength was far superior to the Chinese forces defending the Great Wall but he was equally aware of a trait of our people in refusing to be fully subjugated, so he agreed to accept a set of compromised terms of surrender put forward by the Chinese General in command at the front, historically known as the "Ten Nots." They are: (1) the men may surrender but not the women, (2) the officials but not their attendants, (3) the civilian officials but not the military officers, (4) the elders but not the youngsters, (5) the living but not the dead, (6) the merchants and gentry but not the beg-

Chapter 22 Strong Love for Freedom

gars, (7) the laymen but not the priests or nuns, (8) those who passed imperial examinations but not the ordinary scholars, (9) the living officials but not the dead ones, and finally (10) the head and not the feet. All these "Ten Nots" had to do with their dresses, so throughout the Ts'ing dynasty those on the "Ten Nots" continued to wear their centuries old Chinese dresses. Perhaps a word or two will be required to make the meaning of a "Not" clear between (5) and (9). In (5) when a man was living he had to wear the Manchu dress but at his death he would be robed in the old Chinese style when encoffined. In (9) the dead officials referred to were the images of past officials who had been sainted and were being worshipped in temples. They continued to have their Chinese dresses on. Number (10) referred to the fact that while living men had to use the Manchu headgears they still could wear the regular Chinese shoes.

A glance at these compromised terms of surrender would give us the impression that they would make very little difference in the act of surrender, but Gen. Hung Ch'eng-ch'ou (洪承疇) the Commander of the Chinese forces, must have an insight into the future of our people in our eternal struggle for freedom. The "Nots" apparently had very little influence in the public affairs of the nation buy they constituted the main line of resistance in continuously reminding our people of the loss of their freedom, since they made up the bulk of the population.

Moreover, none of the rulers of this dynasty had developed into a despot. As a matter of fact they proved to be both benevolent and wise and had made use of the Chinese talents in governing the people. Not only important ministerial posts were filled by Chinese but the majority of the civilian posts in the provinces were given to the Chinese. Many attempts were made by patriotic Chinese aiming to overthrow the Manchu yoke. The best known was the Taiping Rebellion in the middle of the last century. Starting from the South in Kwangtung and Kwangsi the so-called rebel forces swept up to the Yangtze basin, but due to internal disorganization it was broken up and crushed with the help of western mercenaries of whom General Gordon was an outstanding character.

At this period China was facing a great danger from the Powers of Europe which were then pursuing a policy of acquiring colonies all over the world. The Spanish and Portuguese were in the forefront followed by the French and British. Towards the end of last century a plan was laid for the partition of China. It went as far as a "shadow" plan, known at that time as "the sphere of influence." Fortunately for our country a wiser counsel prevailed among the European Powers not to carry out the plan as the result of the Boxer uprising in 1900 aimed at the extermination of all Westerners doing business or spreading the Christian religion in China. The American Secretary of State John Hays (Hay) was given the credit for this wise counsel. As this great danger of partition was over, the anger of our people was turned against the Manchu rulers for their inefficiency in bringing about a more modern system of government. As a result the centuries old system of imperial examination was abolished and modern schools were started throughout the country. Thousands of students were sent abroad to acquire this modern knowledge. In Japan alone we had over ten thousand students studying in the Japanese schools, Japan being the first Asian country to adopt western culture and industrial development.

These students became later the sinew of strength in renewing our fight for freedom. Dr. Sun was the prime mover in organizing a political machine aimed at the overthrow of the Manchus once for all. He traveled widely in those countries where our students went and enlisted their support. The result was the successful 1911 Revolution which brought about the final success in regaining our freedom.

This Revolution is more than a mere political upheaval to bring about the downfall of a dynasty and to regain political freedom for our people. It is also the harbinger of economic and social reforms. The important point I wish to emphasize here is our strong love for freedom.

Chapter 23

Spreading of Christianity in China

Christianity came to China rather recently as compared with Buddhism and Mohammedanism while Taoism and Confucianism originated in China. Although the last to come it has made a phenomenal increase in numbers among our people. As we are rather tolerant towards the various religions and are quite strong in our love for freedom, there has never been any opposition to the spreading of Christianity on religious grounds and no ban has ever been put on it on political grounds. Christian missionaries of any nationality have been freely admitted to China and may establish themselves in any locality in the country. Occasionally there have been incidences of persecution or even bloodshed due to misunderstandings between them and the people they came into contact. Many missionaries lost their lives in North China during the Boxer Outbreak when the Manchu Court was misled by the slogan put forward by the Boxers: "Uphold the Ts'ing dynasty and destroy the foreigners." I have alluded to it in a former chapter that were it not for the wisdom and courage of the three men in the Foreign Office when an order of the Court was wired through that office to all the provincial governors of the country by substituting the word "protection" for "destruction" of all foreigners in China, it would have been an even greater massacre of foreigners throughout the country. These men paid their lives for their brave action. Indeed they died in order to save others and the others happened to be "aliens" from other lands. But it is a case of high patriotism as well as a strong sense of justice. They felt that innocent people should not be massacred en masse and that such an action would only lower the standard of civilization in the eyes of the world.

My personal attitude towards religion is in line with the usual Chinese attitude and believe [*sic*] strongly for absolute freedom in the choice of one's faith. The more as I ponder over this vital question in a man's life, the more I am convinced that the goal of life is to conform our will to that of the Supreme Being, the Creator of life and of the whole universe. Our journey in this world is a mere passage towards Him. There are different ways leading to Him as taught by the founders of the principle religions of the world. The most important thing is that whatever road we may choose to follow we must follow it faithfully and prayerfully seeking to know His will in every stage in our journey towards Him.

I was born in a Christian family, so I was put on the "Christian" road very early in my life. As all children go the way their parents go, I followed them along that road. In fact my grandmother was the first in the family to embrace Christianity together with my father who lost his father while still a boy. My father had an elder sister and a younger brother when his father died, so grandmother was looking after them and saw to it that they all followed the "Christian" road faithfully.

Being the fifth child of my parents I was thrown into the arms of my grandmother at an early stage in my life. My father was then the pastor of the church adjoining our residence and mother was busy over her household chores, so I spent most of my child life in the company of my grandmother. One day when I woke up I found her kneeling by my bed and began to wonder what she was doing. Finally curiosity got the better of me and I got up and patted on her shoulder and called "Grandma" in a very low voice. She opened her eyes, motioned me to kneel by her side and told me to close my eyes. Then she began to speak as if to someone in the room. Being anxious to know who the person was, I opened my eyes and began to look around the room. My movements, although quite slight, must have attracted her attention. She got up and holding me by the hand sat down in a chair. I thought she was going to scold me for disobedience, but instead she told me about God our Heavenly Father and the importance to have daily contact with Him by making prayers. Then she told me to repeat the Lord's prayer with her. That marked the beginning of my Christian life in a conscious way. The remark she made to me when I decided to go to North China to study at the age of fourteen that she would remember me in her daily prayers had reenforced the first statement she made to me in our first prayer togeth-

Chapter 23 Spreading of Christianity in China

er on the importance of having daily contact with God.

This enjoinment of my grandmother's has helped me to overcome difficulties in the carrying out of my work that has been assigned to me in the various fields I have been engaged in. It is also a source of inspiration not only to lighten the burden of my work but also to find enjoyment in doing it. From my own experience I began to understand why the Christian missionaries have shown so much zeal and enthusiasm in their work. Thereby I deduced why Christianity has spread so far and wide among the nations of the whole world.

From a handful of men whom Jesus had personally chosen, to whom He gave His parting injunction: "Go ye therefore, and teach all nations, baptizing them in the name of the Father and of the Son, and of the Holy Ghost," we have at the present moment hundreds of millions of men and women throughout the whole world to acknowledge the Christian faith by the emblem of baptism. Their faith has been sustained by their daily contact with God through prayers.

I have always maintained that one must have absolute freedom in the choice of one's religion but coupled with it the absolute necessity of embracing a religion in one's life. Besides being endowed with a body and a mind we have also that infinite attribute of a soul just as one's body must be sustained by food, exercise and care and his mind improved by knowledge and education, so his soul must be renewed by his daily contact with its source, the Spirit of God.

I am a strong believer in the Christian faith, not because I was born in a Christian family, being much influenced naturally by my grandmother and parents. It is the result of personal observation and study of the effect of Christianity upon one's life. At the same time I am not in favour of proselytizing the followers of other religions. We should instead concentrate our attention on those who have no religion. They are people who are traveling through their journey of life without a guide and even the most intelligent, endowed with a wonderful mind, would find themselves at the end of their journey on earth a blind alley leading nowhere. When a person practices a different form of worship and derives satisfaction or consolation in his soul, we should not interfere with it so long as he is leading an upright way of life, striving to be good and to do good. He may call his God by a different name, whether it be Tao or Heaven, or Buddha or Allah we know he is worshipping the same Supreme Being as we Christians do. One and all we should strive to know His will and to conform our lives to it.

The "Christian" road towards God has appealed to me because of its positive nature. We are commissioned to go out to the world to do good, to do something for others so that they could be better in mind, in body and in soul. This is much more effective than the negative attitude of not doing to others what we would not have them do to us. As a boy my contact with the missionaries was of a very superficial nature, being presented to them occasionally when they came to our home to visit our grandmother and parents. I only noticed the difference in appearance, particularly the colour of their hair and the form of their dresses. Most of them were able to speak our Ningpo dialect and so were able to carry on conversation with our folks who knew nothing or only a few words in English. To us children they were only "foreign devils," a term commonly used by our people referring to the missionaries in our midst. They impressed us though as being quite nice people.

My first active contact with a western man was the President of Peiyang University, Dr. C. R. Tenney. He was chosen by our government to head the first institution of learning ever established in China along modern lines. The students whom he had collected by competitive examinations in Shanghai and Hong Kong were only qualified to study in the Preparatory Department of the institution by the end of 1895. For the first time in China our youths were given an opportunity to study physics and chemistry, higher mathematics, geology and other sciences leading on to civil, railway and mechanical engineering. There was also a school for law.

But it was not this plan of modern education, most valuable as it was, that had revolutionized the lives of these youths. The most vital contribution which Dr. Tenney had made was his insistence on having strong bodies as the foundation of an educated mind. At that time physical strength was considered as being vulgar, unsuited to the dignity of a scholar. So most of the boys who came to Peiyang were weak and effeminate, wearing long gowns with delicate hands tapering in shapely finger nails. To overcome this handicap, he instituted two revolutionary requirements, gymnastic exercises and drill, as part of the curriculum of their daily work. No student was allowed to move up to a higher grade unless he was able not only to pass his educational examinations but also his physical tests. There was naturally a great reluctance shown by the students at the beginning but later, as they began to enjoy better health, they went to these exercises with great enthusiasm. They laid aside their long gowns and cut short their pointed nails. At first they were given wooden rifles and appeared on the drill ground in their short coats and trousers. Genuine rifles and uniforms were later issued to them and they rivalled in giving a smart appearance in their parade.

Then came along the Y. M. C. A. work among our students. I was quite impressed with a very tall man by the name of W. D. Lyon. He must be over six feet. At the outset we did not know why he came to us so regularly and was on hand to give us help in our studies or our games and yet not on the teaching staff. We soon learned that he had a mission and that was to give help where it was needed in our mind, body or soul. For the first time we saw that triangle, the symbol of the Y. M. C. A. Movement. In our classroom the triangle has always been with a broad base while the other two sides converging on a point at the top. But the Y. M. C. A. triangle has the point below with the base on the top. The two sides represent a man's body and mind with the base on the top representing a man's soul. A year or so later he was replaced by another Y. M. C. A. worker in R. R. Gailey. He was not only as tall as Mr. Lyon but was almost twice as heavy. Both of them were very popular with the students. Soon thereafter a building was found near our University and I believe that was the first city Y. M. C. A. ever founded in China.

Years later we came into contact with another Y. M. C. A. worker by the name of F. S. Brockman. Before we were formally presented to him at a reception given in his honour, I thought he must be another giant but we found he was of normal size and height. However he proved to be a giant in his mind and soul as I came to know more and more of him in subsequent years in our frequent contact.

The reason why I give an account of these men here is to find out their motive of coming to a land almost entirely unknown to them far from their own country. Dr. Tenney first came out to China also as a missionary. As he was deeply interested in education in his missionary work, his name came to the knowledge of a high Chinese official, Mr. Sheng Hsuan-hwai (盛宣懷) who later became a state minister. Mr. Sheng was a pioneer in promoting modern education and it was he who persuaded our government to found the new institution of learning of Peiyang University at Tientsin. He appointed Dr. Tenney as its first President. Among the first to graduate from this seat of learning is Dr. Wang Chung-hui, the world renowned jurist, who is still holding today the President of the Judicial Yuan in the Chinese government. The work of the Young Men's Christian Association is so well-known throughout the world as to require any analysis into the motive of its workers who are generally known by the title of Secretaries. Although he is the man at the helm of the organization he hides himself behind a board of directors with its chosen President to represent and lead it. He is there only to serve and to guide young men on the path of active service for their growth in mind, body and soul.

This type of active service made a very deep impression on the student body at the University and many of them enrolled in the Bible classes conducted by the Y. M. C. A.. Subsequently they embraced the Christian religion as their "road" towards the Supreme Being. I am sure that the work of other missionaries in other parts of China must have made similar impressions on our people throughout the country, judging by the rapid increasing of Christians in the country. The work of such well-known Christian educational institutions as St. John's in Shanghai, Lin-Nam in Canton, Yenching in Peking and others must have accelerated the growth of Christianity in China. Christian Hospitals and Medical Schools established in so many centre [sic] in China have contributed their share in the spreading of the Christian religion in the country. It is the positive nature of the Christian religion which I believe will eventually be the dominant religion in China. Taoism, Confucianism and Mohammedanism will remain as they are and have been while Buddhism will decrease in number.

Chapter 24

Freedom versus Communism

As I am writing this book it looks as though China is hopelessly divided between two forces of political power. The one on the mainland is controlled by the communists backed up by the all-powerful Russian brand of communism, while National China is holding on to freedom on a small island — Taiwan. In fact it is quite a large island although in appearance it looks small when put in contrast to the huge mainland, but it is a strong citadel for freedom. Being a link among a string of islands from Japan in the north to the Philippines in the south, it stands for the defence of freedom in the east around the Pacific Ocean joining with the Southeast Asian countries, the Bagdad pact nations of the Middle-West and the North Atlantic Treaty Organization of Western Europe. I will deal here only with the part that National China has to play in winning this global war, which might be claimed by future historians as the Third World War. It is neither a cold war nor a hot war. We might say it has been both: a cold-hot war.

No one could put his finger at the exact time when this war was started and it is my belief that it would be as difficult to point at the right moment when it is to be ended. The First World War and the Second World War had their exact beginnings and endings. There has been no Declaration of War in the present global struggle and it is bound to be ended without any Declaration of Peace. It is my opinion that just as China had played an important part in starting this global warfare she is to play a similar important part in ending it.

When the Hitler-Mussolini-Japanese Jingo pact was completely smashed by the end of 1945, it was generally believed that that great world war would end all future wars. How little did the world statesmen then realize that the Second World War was only ended in so far as hot war was concerned. Soon thereafter and without any marked actions, it was turned into a cold-hot warfare which has now continued for over a decade and will only be concluded when the idea of state socialism has run out its course as was the case with the experience in China before the Christian era.

China is now in the grip of a life and death struggle between freedom and communism. This struggle began years before the Japanese surrender at the conclusion of the Second World War. Ever since our success in overthrowing the Manchu dynasty and the founding of a Chinese Republic, the aim of the Revolution was to set up a government of the people, by the people and for the people. In other words it was not merely aiming at the regaining of our freedom from an alien yoke but also to regain that exercise of freedom which our people have always endeavored to maintain throughout the centuries. One of our bitterest enemies against freedom has been the concept and practice of state socialism.

To many people state socialism is conceived as a recent system of government supposed to have been the brain child of Marx, nursed by Lenin and Trosky [Trotsky], and grown up in Russia being invigorated by Stalin. It is far-fetched. State socialism has been long known in China. In fact many attempts have been made to make it work. I will mention only two instances of such attempts before the present one that is being pushed so vigorously on the mainland of China under the name of Socialist Republic of China, dubbed generally as Communist China by the world. Together with Russia and her satellites in Europe, it forms a block of Socialist States threatening world freedom.

The best known attempt was made by a resolute statesman by the name of Shang Yang (商鞅) who flourished under the [sic] dynasty (time) [sic] B. C. He felt there was too great a chasm between the landlords and the farmers in their financial status. He instituted a new system of equalizing the possession of land known in history as the Well-Land system. The Chinese character for a well is thus 井, pronounced Ching which we might call a "Two-Double Ten," in Chinese means Ten. All arable land had to be turned over to the state to be farmed out to the people with nine squares, thus 田, one to each family but only to eight families. The central square was to be reserved for the common use of the eight families. This appeared to be most equitable in theory and was heartily endorsed by the people.

180

Chapter 24 Freedom versus Communism

However, when it was put into practice it would not work as by nature it could not work. To begin with, no two lots of land could ever be equally fertile or have equal facility for the supply of water. Then, no two families could have the same level of brain or brawn, or could practise the same amount of foresight in spending their incomes. In the short space of nine years the lofty theory of equalization was blown up to pieces. The people got so angry that they put nine strong ropes around the body of the disillusioned statesman and pulled by nine strong horses in nine different directions, he died in a manner that has remained most unusual in the execution of a criminal in the history of any nation. Thus ended one attempt of putting state socialism into practice.

Another Chinese statesman tried it in quite a different form under the Sung dynasty (A. D.) [sic] by the name of Wang An-shih (王安石). He used much milder methods in his efforts to practice state socialism but the object was the same to bring about equalization in the distribution of wealth among the people. For twenty seven years and under two Emperors he toiled for the realization of his objective. In a way he was more successful than Shang Yang in that several of his reform measures were tolerated by the people but at the end the result was the same. Our people preferred freedom to state control of their business and financial activities.

One more attempt is being made now by the communist regime in China. Under the impulse of apparent success of the Russian regime since its revolution of 1917 there sprang up a strong band of determined men who would wish to fish in the troubled waters of China for political power, during the war between China and Japan. Since the latter's invasion first in the Three Northeastern Provinces of China and later marched its forces along the Pacific coast as far south as Canton. The Nationalist government of China had to move to the mountain fastness of Western China. The Communist Gorilla [Guerrilla] bands were in name also fighting against the Japanese but used subtle means to keep their forces together and to have a hold on the affection of the China people. After the collapse of Japan in 1945 their leaders did not disdain to proceed to Chungking for a meeting with the National leaders with an American in the person of General Marshall, then Secretary of State. It was a very clever move. Both our National government and the American government were absolutely fooled by them. They were waiting for an opportunity to pounce upon the National forces if any move should be made by the National government which would disillusion the people. Exactly, such an opportunity came when the National government appointed officials to take over the provincial and city governments vacated by the Japanese. These officials instead of befriending the people, assumed the role of conquerors and practiced the maxim: "to the victors belong the spoils," so much so that in less than two years the National forces crumbled like wooden houses before an avalanche of snow when Communist armies marched down south from the north, forcing the National government to find finally a foothold on the tiny island of Taiwan.

Taiwan had been resorted to as the last resort of many a vanishing dynasty on several occasions, the last instance being the exploits of Cheng Ching-kung (鄭成功), better known in history as Koxinga. He led a small force for the defence of the Ming dynasty to Taiwan where he consolidated his position and ruled it until his own death (years: birth to death) [*sic*]. As there was no leader fit to take over his work, the island was taken over by the Manchu dynasty eventually.

The struggle between the Communist on the mainland and the defenders of freedom on the island has now lasted a full decade. Would the defenders of freedom have the same fate of Cheng Ching-kung's exploits in Taiwan? My answer is a positive No. Casual observers might draw the opposite conclusion, for in resources and men-power the forces for freedom appear to have a very slim chance of winning the struggle, but world conditions nowadays differ very much from those in Cheng Ching-kung's time. Taiwan was then a mere small island, practically unknown to the world, and the forces defending the island were only fighting for their own existence. At the present moment Taiwan forms an important link in the chain of defence against the aggresion [aggression] of communism throughout the whole world while its defenders are motivated by the all sustaining power of fighting for freedom. Those ragged but rugged men fighting under Washington at Valley Forge for the freedom of America were similarly motivated. The defenders of Taiwan are in much better situation than those under Washington. The American Revolutionists had the French contingents to aid them but that could not be compared with the aid given to the Chinese Nationalists in Taiwan by the freedom-loving nations of the World led by Americans. With the American 7th fleet guarding the Pacific with strong armies and air forces ready to join in, the Chinese communists even with their powerful Russian ally would have to think twice before they dare to take any positive action against Taiwan.

But the crucial test in this life and death struggle between state socialism and freedom does not lie so much on the relative strength of the fighting forces. It is in the inherent strength of the two schools of thought — Freedom versus State Socialism. The latter may at times seem destined to win out but inevitably to be crushed by the forces of freedom, as has been repeatedly shown by our history in the several attempts made by the State Socialists in China.

It is significant to note that state socialism has been resorted to only in a country when there is a great disparity between the rulers and the ruled. When the rulers bathed in their wealth while the ruled are in desperate economic needs, such a situation would inevitably lead to state socialism. Promises of equalization in the economic structure of the people would lead them to acquiesce in it, if not directly supporting it.

Let us take a look at Russia at the Kerensky revolution. The Russian rulers under the Czar were certainly rolling in wealth while the Russian peasants were being trodden down by their rulers, the revolution led by Kerensky and others succeeded in breaking down the Czarist regime and might have succeeded in setting up a democratic form of government but the Russian people were not ready for it. State socialism as voiced by Lenin and Trosky [Trotsky] found a ready ear among the populace. The ill gotten wealth of the great landed-property owners would be turned over to the State to be distributed equitably among the people. What a promise and what a prospect! One could easily imagine the readiness of the people to acquiesce in the new regime. I am sure that was how our forefathers felt at the proposal of Shang Yang for his wonderful theory of equal ownership of land under the so called "Well" Land system. I have already explained why it did not work and in spite of the apparent success so far in Russia, it could not work there either in the end. I dare make a prediction that sooner or later state socialism would fail in Russia as it did in China centuries ago. The reason for its temporary success for such a fairly long period is due to the fact that freedom of the Russian people had been so long denied in Russia under the Czarist regime.

It is reasonable for us to make a similar prediction that it could not succeed in China and that the period of its being carried on would last much shorter than in Russia for two reasons. The first is that our people have always struggled successfully for freedom and the second is a corollary of the first, namely it had been tried again and again and failed every time in the past centuries.

Chapter 25

Peering into the Future

I would like to take my readers along for a peep or two into the future of China in particular and of the world in general. What the future holds for us is in the lap of the Gods. It is certainly most difficult for any human being to predict accurately what is in store for us individually, but with the collective fate of a nation or with the general trend of world affairs one may fairly well predict what the future is likely to be. The life of a nation has a much longer history to guide us to form an opinion as to how it is likely to develop into. The same is true with the trend of world situation. Still we could only take peeps at them.

The old adage that history repeats itself furnishes us with a mental telescope through which we could take peeps into the future with greater clarity. History tells us that our people have always put a premium on the value of mental training. It has always been a special privilege of our people. Anyone with sufficient mental ability plus a zeal to pursue knowledge could reach the highest in social or political status. In a primary book for the children there is a significant statement which runs as follows: "in the morning one may be the son of a farmer but in the evening he will ascend to the hall of the Emperor." It is to encourage every boy to study hard so that when he succeeds to pass the imperial examination he will be received by the Emperor himself. The two words "morning" and "evening" are only a poetical expression of the two periods in a man's life. Education has always been in the forefront in the achievements among our people. Hence their high standard of intelligence. It is said that one may pick any urchin on the street without any mark of social standing, he may prove to be an outstanding scholar when given an opportunity to learn. This statement was made by a prominent American missionary who had contributed a good deal to the advancement of modern education in China.

Still, China is one of the countries in the world which has a high percentage of illiteracy even at the present day nearly a half century after the introduction of modern education. The root of it is the low standard of the earning power of our people. Most fathers do not get enough income even to feed and clothe their children. The latter have to start work when quite young thus losing the opportunity of getting education in that golden period of learning.

Besides, the centuries old system of city, provincial and imperial examinations which placed emphasis only on literature and philosophy, had stifled the very aim of education for the mass of our people. To the successful ones, who were able to pass these examinations, every door was open to them for social and political advancement but the unsuccessful ones remained poor in their lives as the traditional church mice. The successful ones were only one in a hundred who went in for these examinations. Moreover, not every one of the successful candidates could get official appointments. While they get a high social status as the Flowers of Education they would also remain poor in their lives. These in turn would discourage their children to seek education, not only because of their great disappointment themselves but because they had no means to give their children such an education.

With the introduction of modern education, the picture took a sharp turn. The boys now have an opportunity to learn something which will enable them to get into the professional and business lines besides government appointments. These in turn will lead them to a much higher standard in life. Some of them have become millionaires while many others have amassed wealth large enough for them to maintain a high standard of living. Science has been the branch of education least known to our people in the last ten or fifteen centuries, although history has shown us that our forefathers did pay much attention to topics like astrology, geology, chemistry, physics and other scientific subjects. For nearly thirty generations they had been closed books to our youths. Yet in only about half-a-century after the introduction of modern education, there are now two Chinese professors who have been recently awarded a Nobel Prize for physics! This goes to show that our people have not lost the high intelligence which our forefathers were endowed with. All these will give us strong stimulus towards our goal of universal education of our people, not only to wipe out that high percentage of illiteracy among our people but also to develop a standard of education on a par with other nations.

Let us take a peep into the future of our country in another direction. Physically speaking we seem to be small in size, soft and weak in limbs, and effeminate in appearance. This was quite a true picture of our people in general only a generation ago. To be able to be classified as a member of the literati has always been the aim in life for our youths. In the old days, though, archery was included in the six "musts" for the training of our youths. That connotates^{connotes} that physical development was considered as important as mental training. Gradually, cultivation of the mind gained a precedence over that of the body so much so that our people had been let to believe that physical strength was a mere mark of vulgarity. No scholar would like to have that stigma on him. The system of examinations initialed by the Court had further advanced this idea until it was considered "nice and decent" for a scholar to wear long gowns and to have delicate hands with pointed finger-nails. Had this idea been practised by our people in all walks of life, we would have been one of the "lost tribes" among the family of nations. But fortunately the bulk of our people have always been tillers of the land, who together with the artisans must use their hands due to the nature of their work. Their hands could not but be rough and without pointed finger-nails. They have helped to maintain the virility of our race.

Nevertheless, our athletes have been found trailing behind those of other countries in physical competitions as witnessed in the games of the International Olympic Committee, held so far. It was in 1896 when Baron Pierre de Coubertin, together with his friends of several nationalities revived the Olympic Games in Greece, the home of the original Olympic Games which had been held from 776 B. C. to 394 A. D. when a decree by Emperor Theodosius I put an end to this athletic as well as religious festival. But in 1896 physical competitive games were even unheard of in China. A system of modern education was just being introduced which had placed physical tests in the curriculum for the students. They were just beginning to put off their long gowns and to cut short their finger-nails. Efforts were made at the beginning of the present century to encourage physical competitive games in the various cities where institutions for modern education existed. A national organization for the promotion of physical games was effected under the leadership of Dr. Chang Po-ling and Mr. William Z. L. Sung, known as the China National Amateur Athletic Federation. The first Olympic Game in which China took part was the Eleventh held in Los Angeles, California, U. S. A. in 1932 when we sent our lonely athlete, Chang-cheng Liu to compete in the 5,000 Metre Run. Although he was our best long distance runner at that time, he was not even able to win a place. This goes to show that athletes are not made in a day. I might add not even in a generation when physical culture was only being introduced in our schools and colleges. The people in general did not even know what games their children were playing.

It is interesting to note the steady physical improvement among the children of our athletes. They usually grow taller and stronger than their parents. It is here where we could use our mental telescope to take another peep into the future of our people on their improvement in health and physical growth.

Important as modern education and physical health are in the life of a nation, we will all agree that the most important is to bring happiness to our people. There are two ways — one is negative and the other is positive. The former deals with relief work for illness, calamity or any adverse circumstances, while the latter is to direct one's mind from a mundane life to a spiritual outlook.

The old adage of "Sweeping the snow in from of your own gate but refrain from meddling with frost on other people's roof" is a warning against interfering with other people's business. But it tends to make people indifferent to the welfare of others. Frost does not do much damage to a roof, so the adage advises us not to meddle with it, but there are matters which are bound to do great harm if they remain unchecked. One could never feel indifferent if a case of cholera breaks out in the home of your neighbour or his house has caught fire. In such circumstances, we should see to it that the patient suffering from cholera be placed in an isolation hospital and to receive proper medical care or we should at once call up the fire brigade to put the fire out. Hence the necessity of promoting Social Welfare work.

This Social Welfare work has been urged and practiced in our country from time immemorial. We have been taught to regard the welfare of other people as our own. The old proverbs as "All within the four seas are brothers" and "Let us render assistance to other peoples' elders as we would to our own and similarly succour their youths as our own," indicate to us how our forefathers have practiced it. So it is not something new. Only in the present day life, there is a tendency for people to live in congested areas thereby creating conditions which have to be carefully watched against any possible disaster. Epidemic outbreak, fire, robbery and street accidents are matters of great concern to the welfare of such communities. Above all, there is always a concentration of poor people in large cities. Due to illness or unemployment, people have been thrown out of work. Whatever may be the cause, the condition of such people should be looked after by the whole communities.

Such being the sentiment of our people vis-à-vis social needs in our communities, we could feel sure that the importance of social welfare work is bound to grow as the needs increase due to modern condition of living in congestion. What is necessary to be done in meeting this situation is to bring about greater efficiency in the carrying out of our social welfare work throughout the country. In most large cities we have organized Kaifong Associations, whose object is to bring assistance to those who stand in need. This organization should be extended to smaller cities and even to rural districts.

Our life upon earth is certainly limited to a very short period. The great psalmist has told us that "the days of our years are three-score years and ten; and if by reason of strength they are four score years, yet is their strength labour and sorrow; for it is soon cut off, and we fly away." In China our poets sing of a long life as that of a hundred years. The same psalmist reminded us that "in the sight of God a thousand years are but as yesterday when it is past, and as a watch in the night." From these two statements we could deduce that although our mundane life is a very short one, our spiritual life is unlimited. A short mundane life to be followed by an eternal spiritual life will certainly inspire us to strive for that most blissful expectation in our mundane life. Here is where religion plays its most important part in our lives.

Of the five great religions of the world China has made two contributions: Taoism and Confucianism. They have contributed their share in guiding our people from life on earth to the eternal spiritual life, leading them towards the Supreme Being. What comfort and happiness they have given us in their great teachings! However, these teachings could only reach a small part of our people, those who have been sufficiently educated to be able to read them and ponder over them. They are couched in highly classical and philosophical language, and are most difficult for the illiterate to understand. Unfortunately before the introduction of modern education in China, the majority of our people have been and are still illiterate. It explains why our people have turned so eagerly to Buddhism and Christianity when they were brought into China. I do not mean that Buddhistic and Christian religions do not have literature of classical and philosophical standard but they have more simple and direct means to convey their teachings to the people at large. Only the well educated could read their literature inasmuch as they read Taoist and Confucianist standard books.

The followers of Buddhism make use of objects which the ordinary people could easily understand. First of all they erect large temples and place in them the images of the great teachers of their religion, the Supreme Buddha and his disciples — not only those who were in personal touch with him but all those in later generations who have achieved greatness in their religion and have been duly sainted. Simple liturgies were sung by the worshippers, burning of candles and incense, and the offerings of food and fruit and flowers. All these outward signs could but direct their thoughts and actions towards a spiritual life.

The same may be said of the practices among the Christians. They also have a tendency to build large churches or cathedrals for their place of worship. They do not have images for worship but a cross, either large or small, is usually hung in front of the audience. It is to remind them of the supreme sacrifice of their Savior for the remission of their sins. The Catholic priests and the clergymen of the English High Church wear robes in conducting religious services more or less as the Buddhist monks do. They also light candles in all their churches and some even burn incense. The reason for such practice is quite obvious. It is to draw their attention to their God whom they worship in spirit. The followers of Mohammed also build mosques more or less similar to the Christian churches or cathedrals. Their form of worship is essentially the same, differing only in minor details.

All religions, however, teach the same central theme of leading human beings on their journey of life on earth towards a living God who was, is and ever shall be, in whose house all the races of the world shall dwell in peace where there shall be no more strife, rancour or warfare due to differences on earth in race, colour or creed. Our people have always maintained the freedom of religious believers. In spite of the fact that those of our forefathers who had the privilege of education had faithfully followed the words of the founders of Taoism and Confucianism to lead their lives on the right Path or Road in life, they would not object to others who began to embrace Buddhism. As the bulk of our people did not have the advantage of classical education, Buddhism gave them greater comfort in life by worshipping some visible objects instead of the invisible Tao, a word which actually means a road or path. This explains why Buddhism soon found its way into most of the homes in China.

Christianity was brought to China at a much later period. Catholic priests were the first to teach the Christian faith in China, soon after the Christian nations of Europe came into contact with China in the sixteenth century A. D.. Europe was then under Roman Catholicism before any of the Christian bodies in Europe actually broke away from Roman communion to be designated thereafter as the Protestant branch of the Christian faith. Morrison was the first Protestant missionary to teach the Christian faith to our people, followed soon after by thousands of Protestant missionaries in the nineteenth century, not only from the countries in Europe but also from a young Republic in America. By the end of that century the Protestant missionaries were preeminently American. To us we take very little note over this division between the Catholics and Protestants. We do not even take sides among the followers of other religions. We believe that all religions have the same ultimate goal — to lead humanity towards their Creator, who may be called by a different name in each religion. It is to guide us in the path of righteousness and to give us a richer and happier life on earth.

It is my profound belief that China will prove to be the land where not only Catholics and Protestants will heartily cooperate with each other, but the followers of all religions will seek concerted action in the main theme of promoting human happiness by leading mankind from this mundane life to the spiritual life with their Creator.

Let us now take a look at the future of the world situation. History is a record of man's achievements. Without man's power of reasoning, researching and realization of ideas and ideals, this world, beautiful as it is in natural settings, would have remained as it was in Adam's Garden. Besides substantial buildings for homes and work, clothes to keep warm and comfortable, and a thousand and one other items which mark the achievements of mankind, the world is adorned with great constructions that have been called Great Wonders. At the same time history is a record of wars, starting from isolated small tribal fightings on to national and racial warfare, and finally to the great conflicts in modern history known as World Wars. There is no doubt that man will continue to make great achievements in making this world a more beautiful, comfortable and happy place to live in. There is no comparison between the present age with the stone age but even between the present century and the last. What a difference do we find in home comfort, in transportation, in medical care and treatment, in telephonic and telegraphic communications, in listening to voices and viewing scenes from afar off, ad infinitum. [sic] But will mankind ever abandon war as a means of settling their differences?

The World War II was dubbed by many statesmen of world fame as the war to end all future wars. Does it? Apparently it does not, for the world has not even finished with that Great War. There has been a prolonged cold war now over a decade after the surrender of the forces under Hitler, Mussolini, and the Japanese jingoists. What an irony to imagine that the three nations above mentioned, against whom the world forces for freedom once were mobilized and pitched, are now actively on the side of the Free World against a power that was once an ally of the Free World! Yet, such is the fact. Then, is it logical for us to expect that there will be no more future wars to debase mankind? The apparent logical answer is that in the future there will be wars as they have been in the past.

I have used the word "apparent" most advisedly. I have solid reasons for my belief, as I peer into the future world situation through my historic telescope, that there will be less likelihood of world wars as mankind continues to improve the means of destruction through warfare. The most potent factor is the growing desires of the nations of the world to better understand each other's social, economical and political situations and to bring about better cooperation between them.

It is a truism that when two persons are both well-armed, they are less likely to come to blows for each has to consider his own safety first. The present world situation is just like such two individuals. The two sides of the present cold war are both well armed for each other's extinction. It is not a question of victory or defeat for one or the other but a possible extinction of both. With a Hydrogen bomb that could wipe off a whole city, carried by a missile that could travel thousands of miles and hit on a spot as accurately as a bullet on a bull's eye with a rifle, is certainly a weapon not to be trifled with. Both sides in the present struggle between freedom and state socialism are armed with such deadly weapons. This is exactly the reason why this cold war has been prolonged so long. Thousands of millions of dollars have to be spent each year for the production of these weapons, some of which have to be discarded and replaced by still deadlier weapons. How long could this cold war continue without bringing about total exhaustion on one side or the other? The answer to this question furnishes the key to the present world situation.

We have many examples of this kind of life and death struggle in history. I will take the case of the American Civil War in the middle of the last century, known generally as the War for Freedom for the negro slaves in the Southern States of the American Republic. It is a typical case of struggle between freedom and slavery. Thousands upon thousands of negroes, either captured, lured or bought in Africa, were brought to the United States and sold in the slave market. The Northern States were largely engaged in industries and trades and had very little use for slaves, so the bulk of these negroes found a ready market in the Southern States to be engaged in the farms in a region that is hot in temperature. These negro slaves were like chattels to be bought and sold in the slave markets. At first they behaved like dumb animals and so for many generations slave owners and slaves lived in peace. It is in human nature to develop a sense of injustice when certain human beings were treated like animals. Even harsh treatments of animals would evoke public censure. Naturally, harsh treatments of slaves would arouse a much greater public censure, particularly by that section of the American people who never owned slaves. In time this sense of injustice grew in intensity so much so that it became a national issue on the question of slave ownership. The election of Abraham Lincoln to the presidency of the American Republic showed such a marked tendency in favour of the abolition of slavery in America that the Southern States decided to secede from the Union. This brought about the four years of Civil War and was ended only on the exhaustion of the Southern Confederacy.

I have chosen this case to show what is to be expected in the present world struggle between Freedom and State Socialism. It is a gigantic struggle. It is now in the cold war stage and may develop into a hot war but it seems to me that State Socialism may be brought to the stage of utter exhaustion before the flare up of a hot war. In either case we could get a fairly good view of what is to come in the future.

This war of exhaustion is a typical example of the struggle between those who believe in freedom and the others who want the world to accept their view through thick or thin. The Northern States in America, for instance, while condemning slavery would tolerate the slave owners in Southern States to continue their owning slaves. In times the slaves themselves began to notice the vast difference between freedom and slavery, so they began to look for opportunities to flee from slavery to a land of freedom in ever increasing numbers in spite of the harsh measures undertaken by their masters to keep them in bondage. Due to the growing public censure on slavery on the one hand and the increasing tendency for slaves to flee from their bondage on the other, the slaves owners felt that the only way to keep their slaves was to declare secession from the Union of the American States, thereby bringing about the Civil War. The same situation exists today between the free world and the countries now controlled by the Communists. Ever increasing numbers of people are fleeing from the countries under the rule of communists to any neighbouring country where freedom is assured and practiced. The time is bound to come, and that not too far away, the communistic states would feel it necessary to make a similar declaration of secession from the family of nations. The cold war that has been in existence during the last ten years would then turn into a hot war with the inevitable result of any struggle between freedom and slavery. I would echo the sentiments of Abraham Lincoln that America could not be half free and half slave. So this world could not be half free and half slave either.

編者略歴

服 部 龍 二（はっとり　りゅうじ）

1968年，東京都に生まれる。京都大学法学部卒業。神戸大学大学院法学研究科単位修得退学。博士（政治学）。現在，中央大学総合政策学部准教授（日本外交史・東アジア国際政治史専攻）。著作に『東アジア国際環境の変動と日本外交 1918-1931』（有斐閣，2001年），『幣原喜重郎と二十世紀の日本──外交と民主主義』（有斐閣，2006年），『広田弘毅』（中公新書，2008年）など。

王正廷回顧録 Looking Back and Looking Forward
中央大学学術図書（70）

2008年8月10日　初版第1刷発行

編　者　服　部　龍　二
発行者　玉　造　竹　彦

発行所　中　央　大　学　出　版　部
東京都八王子市東中野742番地1
郵便番号　192-0393
電話　042(674)2351　FAX 042(674)2354

© 2008　Ryuji HATTORI　　　印刷・大森印刷／製本・法令製本
ISBN978-4-8057-4143-6

本書の出版は中央大学学術図書出版助成規程による